THE MEDITATIVE FISHERMAN

The Meditative Fisherman

Lifetime Reflections on Fly Fishing

BRYAN ARCHER

Illustrated by Emma O'Connor-Bray

Ensemble Publishing

CONTENTS

To Ann,

Who never baulked once at my requests to go fishing and, indeed, encouraged me when I appeared to be getting twitchy if I hadn't wet a line for a little while.

Travel is fatal to prejudice, bigotry and narrow-mindedness, and many of our people need it sorely on these accounts. Broad, wholesome, charitable views of men and things cannot be acquired by vegetating in one little corner of the earth all one's lifetime.

MARK TWAIN

INTRODUCTION

In the grounds of the Maudsley Hospital, a psychiatric institution in South London, a man holds a fly rod with a length of flyline extended before him. At the end of the flyline another man, about ten years older, is running towards the man with the rod, shouting to him to retrieve the flyline so that any slack is eliminated between them. He then runs away from the rod bearer, shouts at him to release more flyline and, conforming to that request, the flyline is taut once again.

In neither instance did I allow enough slack for the trout to throw the hook and escape. I was the man with the rod, and so I began to learn how to 'play' a trout. The trout was Terry, my brother-in-law. He was somewhat older than me, an experienced fly fisherman and a psychiatrist practicing at the Maudsley Hospital. People walking the footpath close by might have reasoned that this was normal behaviour at a mental institution, but I couldn't stop guffawing as we acted this out for twenty minutes or so. Terry couldn't figure out what was so funny.

We had arrived for a two-day visit when he pointed out that, although coarse fish generally just swam into the waiting net, trout weren't so obliging. He was working the next day, but was keen for me to experience what a trout would do once hooked, so I found myself in the grounds of the hospital. Terry's enthusiasm was infectious, undaunted by his exertions and his shouts of "too slow, Bryan," or "you gave it too much welly". I learned that no bend of the rod meant the slack flyline would enable a trout to engineer a release, and too much bend of the rod meant that the leader of nylon was under enormous pressure, and there was some likelihood of the hook coming away from it as it broke, releasing the fish.

———————————

There was a time when I wasn't a fisherman, though now I can hardly remember not being one. I was not lucky enough to have an adult to introduce me to maggots, worms or bread, so I was ignorant that these baits caught a variety of fish. My entry into fishing didn't come until my mid-twenties, coarse fishing for roach and dace. Boys need to experience a fish on their line – then they are as hooked as the fish, and are eager to return. Catch nothing for a few outings, and with their low boredom threshold, excuses start to form on their lips. For me, taking it up later, fishing wasn't just about netting fish, but also served as a stress-relieving activity, away from work and family. Fishing was then the largest participatory sport in the UK, with millions of anglers using what leisure they had to wet a line. Today, that isn't the case – many more choices of leisure activities abound, games and electronic gizmos have taken over a great deal of leisure time, and sadly going to a riverbank or pond with a rod doesn't seem to cut it any more for most people, especially the young.

I became a fly fisherman, but many anglers specialise, some as carp fishermen, others targeting pike or other species. Others take to sea fishing. Coarse fishing or sea fishing fishermen have a variety of skills and use various 'baits', both animal and mineral. Having done some coarse fishing, I found that although relaxing, watching a float or a bite indicator was not very fulfilling, and I became a bit bored with it. Fly fishing provides a different approach, including choice of fly, what depth and therefore what flyline to use, what speed of retrieve to contemplate, and some knowledge of nature. It feels like a more cerebral method of fishing.

One thing common to all of us is that catching fish was always more than we expected, but not exactly more than we had hoped for. I never took to the catching of roach, chubb and other coarse fish species, but maybe if the eels had left me alone (I hated catching the damn things) I might have persevered. Instead I took up fishing with a fly at the behest of a work colleague who didn't want to look an ass learning to cast a fly on a flyline, and so talked me into joining him.

We were great friends, John and I. He was into carp fishing, and was one of those anglers who ate, slept and talked carp. As we were supping pints at our post-work pub, he suddenly and surprisingly suggested that together we should try fly fishing. John was a salesman, with the gift of the gab, and I found myself being talked into buying one of these beginner packages that tackle dealers used to sell. It had everything, even some flies for a little outlay, and we were good to go.

Fishing had always appeared to me to be a boring enterprise — just watching a float or bite indicator until something happens — and it was not something I had ever planned on doing. We turned up at a local trout lake to ineptly thrash the water with our flylines.

Then I hooked my first ever trout, a rainbow, no more than a pound, that took a white baby doll fly. I never really thought that I would catch anything, so I ran up the bank shouting to John "what do I do? What do I do?". Mightily amused, he netted it, and it was mine — my very first trout!

I knew then I had a long way to go before I could be called a fly fisherman. John didn't really take to it and went back to his carp. In time he was promoted to a post several hundred miles away and became, in the end, just someone on my Christmas card list, but I have a lot to thank him for in introducing me to this wonderful sport. I have been lucky enough to have had some marvellous experiences in some wonderful places, that might never have happened without that first rainbow trout.

Author John Geirach sums up fly fishing perfectly:

Fly fishing is solitary, contemplative, misanthropic, scientific in some hands poetic in others, and laced with conflicting aesthetic considerations. It's not even clear if catching fish is actually the point.

This sums up the many reasons why I, and many others, feel the need to go fishing, and shows the schism that exists in the makeup of every fly fisherman. Fishing has been an escape when I needed one, such as when I was made redundant, with a young family to support. Leaving all the ramifications that flooded my consciousness behind, I took refuge in fishing. There is an enduring mystery to what will occur when you cast a fly into the river or lake. You never know what will happen. You hope, and if you catch a fish, you hope you can catch another — you can never catch too many.

Some are 'born' fishermen, then there are those who have to work at it, and I was the latter. When another fisherman compliments me, saying that I am a good fisherman, I just reply "I have fished for so many years now, I couldn't be otherwise." In *A Fly Rod of Your Own*, John Gierach sums up the paradoxes involved in becoming a competent fly fisherman with his usual cogency:

> There are few broad strokes in fly fishing. It's all specific details strung together in a precise order: too many details to think about, really, but over time you wear neural pathways and the process resolves itself into something like instinct. This happens gradually and comes from nothing but repetition. There are no shortcuts, and the hunt for shortcuts only distracts you from the business of letting the craft become second nature. Eventually, you lose track of how little you think about it until someone asks you to teach them how to fly fish and you do have to think about it.

Perhaps it is appropriate that I am using someone else's words to explain why this book of mine isn't a 'how-to' book about becoming a fly fisherman, as really, the only way in achieving this is to go out and start the process and begin to connect with this absorbing sport. Throughout the ages, angling literature has produced many outstanding classics – some so evocative that you can almost feel that you are part of the experience. Some are based on the author's own life, others are fictional, like *The Old Man and the Sea* by Ernest Hemingway, and then there are the books which are there to teach you what to do to be a successful fisherman. This book doesn't fit neatly into one of these categories, in fact I'll be discussing not just fishing, but the some of the thoughts that my fishing expeditions have led me to, or helped me explore. I must add, many of the original 'thoughts' are not mine; I could never be termed an original thinker, but I have recognised that other writers on so many diverse subjects have produced extraordinary stuff – and although not mine, I will admit to believing in much of it.

I regard myself as very privileged to enjoy a sport that I have undertaken in many beautiful parts of the world. I cannot think of a pastime that can be executed with such sublime simplicity or with such complicated operations of thought. After fishing, a problem or dilemma that was, beforehand, foremost in your mind, seems to be resolved. I have gone fishing only with a desire to spend time on the water. At other times I have beaten myself up, trying to execute a strategy that could, would or should work, but doesn't. Mindsets don't ordain success or failure, but the most successful fishermen aren't prone to overthinking. Fishing has introduced me to the crueler side of humanity's nature, that I have to square with myself. We are not, after all, cuddling cute kittens or doing good works, but trying to catch one of god's creatures with a hook. And we could not pursue this wonderful pastime if we didn't have the consent of our family, particularly our spouses or partners, and are indebted to them for their understanding of why we just have to go fishing.

One of the earliest recorded entries of an artificial fly for fishing that I am aware of was written by Claudius Aelianus, who lived from 175AD-235AD. Aelianus wrote seventeen books titled *De Natura Animalium* (*On the Nature of Animals*), a curious collection of stories of natural history. In the seventeenth book, he records that "in a river in Thessalonica, flies seek their food over the river but do not escape the observation of the fish swimming below. When the fish observes a fly on the surface, it swims quietly up and opens its mouth and gently gulps down the fly like a wolf carrying off a sheep from the fold or an eagle a goose from the farmyard". With the limited materials the ancients had in those days, they nevertheless produced an imitation that worked. Aelianus further records that "fishermen fastened crimson red wool around a hook and fixed onto the wool two feathers which grew under a cock's wattle which was the colour of wax. They throw this snare onto the water and the fish attracted and maddened by the colour, comes straight at it, thinking it would gain a dainty mouthful. However, when it opens its jaws it is caught by the hook and enjoys a bitter repast as a captive".

Some 1200 years were to pass before a significant account was published about fly fishing, written by a nun, a Prioress of Sopwell Nunnery near St Albans, called Juliana Berners. Titled 'A treatyse of fysshynge with an angle', it was part of *The Boke of St Albans* published in 1486. Amongst other fishing-related subjects, it includes the crafting of artificial flies. Dame Juliana Berners was born in 1388 of a high-born family, and certainly would have hunted and fished before took the veil – *if* she lived. Historians are still unable to verify whether the angling nun actually existed, as records from that period are sketchy and some are missing. Unlike Claudius Aelianus, whose life was well documented through his writings and views on Greco-Roman life, particularly his work relating to Pliny the Elder, Dame Juliana Berners life is simply not written down. A classic fudge ensues about the authorship of the book: that there is no evidence to say that the first book on angling was written by a woman – when of course, the contrary is also the case.

There is no 'real' record of her existence, yet she could indeed be the author of 'A treatyse of fysshynge with an angle'. It is possible that an angling, hunting nun was just too improbable for people to believe – but I think if a monk had been credited with that book, there would have been less opposition as to whether he had existed or not, and he would have been given the benefit of the doubt. The legacy of the book, twelve artificial flies – one for every month of the year – are nonetheless real, and notwithstanding modern fly development, if they were used today, they would still be effective in catching fish. The fishing nun is reported to have said: "It will be a true pleasure to see the fair, bright, shining-scaled fishes deceived by your crafty means". Amen to that.

Driven by the new popularity of the sport, the nineteenth and twentieth centuries produced an explosion of fly fishing literature, but it was Izaak Walton's *The Compleat Angler,* first published in1653, that has remained enduringly popular. It has since been reprinted more times than Milton's *Paradise Lost,* which was published just fifteen years later. It's not a how-to book either, but simply a book of prose and verse, a celebration of the art and spirit of fishing – perhaps I have taken some inspiration from him. Walton continued to add to his work over the next twenty-five years with more poems, songs and anecdotes.

Born in 1593, Walton had considerable talents. Initially known as an ironmonger, he trained as a linen draper, then a trade under the auspices of the ironmongers company, and had several shops in London. A Verger and Churchwarden of St Dunstans, he became a friend of John Donne and contributed an elegy to the 1633 edition of Donne's poems. He died aged ninety and is buried in Winchester Cathedral. Despite his biographies of several important people, *The Compleat Angler* remains his masterpiece. It was so popular that Charles Lamb entreated Samuel Taylor Coleridge to read it, saying:

It breathes the very spirit of innocence, purity and simplicity of heart. There are many choice old verses interspersed in it; it would sweeten a man's temper at any time to read it; it would Christianise every discordant angry passion; pray make yourself acquainted with it.

Isaak Walton's influence remains worldwide: there are fly fishing clubs, pubs and hotels named after him in as diverse locations as the Bahamas, Kenya and England; a mountain named for him in the Sierra Nevadas in California; and a Recreational Park in Alaska bearing his name. His name also prefaces a fishing conservation society, and Walton, over 400 years after his death, has been inducted into the American National Fresh Water fishing Hall of Fame. Old Izaak Walton has done well.

Yet the 'act' of fishing doesn't always match Isaak's honeyed words. Fishing can lead you to the depths of despair or the heights of exhilaration, and keeps you hooked with the hormones it produces – usually adrenaline. We might be in a beautiful environment, but can become so self-absorbed and single-minded that this isn't something we always appreciate as we grapple with catching our prey. Writers remind us that fishing should be a noble sport: Norman Maclean, whose father was a minister, wrote, "In our family, there is no clear line between religion and fly fishing"; A.J. McClane reasons more abstractly: "People often ask me why I enjoy fishing, and I cannot explain it to them because there is no reason the way they want reasons described. They are asking a man why he enjoys breathing when he really has no choice but to wonder at its truth". Washington Irving wrote, "There is certainly something in angling that tends to produce a gentleness of spirit and a pure serenity of mind", but I cannot, in all honesty, agree with this last statement. Serenity depends on how successful you have been, and on many of my fishing trips I have displayed very few of these characteristics.

Dry fly fishing is, to me, the most exciting method of fly fishing. It is sometimes immensely frustrating. The fish can appear to 'take' the fly, only for you to lift the rod to find it has turned away at the last moment, or indeed has mouthed and rejected the fly in one quick movement. The father of dry fly fishing was Frederic Halford, born in April 1844 in Birmingham to wealthy Jewish parents, who in due course changed their name from Hyam to Halford. Frederic began fishing aged six, in a local pond near his London home, and took up fly fishing at the age of twenty-four. At thirty-five, he became a member of the exclusive Houghton fly fishers on the River Test, through which he met angler and country gentleman, George Selwyn Marryat, and they became friends. He wrote his first book, *Floating Flies and How to Dress Them*, shortly afterwards, and wanted Marryat to be listed as a co-author. Marryat declined, preferring to remain anonymous. The book was a great success, as were other books Halford wrote, and he is understandably given the title of 'High Priest of the dry fly'. However, Halford's enthusiasm for dry fly fishing — advocating it as the purest form of fly fishing — created a schism in the fly-fishing fraternity. His advocacy of dry fly fishing implied that those fishing with an under-water nymph pattern were using a secondary and inferior technique.

I don't know how I would have spent my leisure time if I hadn't been encouraged to go fishing – maybe I would have taken up golf (though I was no good at it) – it was serendipity that I knew someone persuasive enough to get me to try something that I would otherwise never have done. Granted, my great-uncles worked the trawlers out of Lowestoft when the town was a location for a huge fleet, but that was a different kind of fishing. My mother, who was a Lowestoft girl, told me she would go aboard one of the trawlers with her brother to 'set the compass'. My grandfather arranged the lodgings of the Scottish herring girls as they moved around the east coast from Aberdeen to Great Yarmouth, following the herring as they migrated in enormous shoals from Scotland in the spring, down to the coast of East Anglia in the Autumn. The herring girls would be there, ready to gut and pre-serve them when the trawlers landed this bounty. Now all the herring have gone.

There is a fly which I have used successfully in New Zealand (where I first came across it) called Serendipity, named for the faculty for making fortunate discoveries by accident. I love just listening to the sound of this spoken word, which conjures up, in its five syllables, optimism and hope. How much I have to thank serendipity for! I'm not alone – many people find partners, make connections, by serendipitous 'accidents'. Without it I wouldn't have met my partner, Ann, or experi-enced all the joy that we have shared. Serendipity gave me a good hand: Anne never complained about a hobby that became all-enveloping, both in terms of time and, to a lesser extent, money.

It is hard for me to accept that one day I will be unable to go fishing — almost unimaginable, though I know it will come. Yet I also know it has enriched my life immeasurably, as it has done for fishermen through the millennia.

TACKLE

FLIES

Flies, with various confections, materials, tied around a bare hook, are made to imitate insects, both aquatic and terrestrial, which fish feed on. Flies are also tied to resemble small fish that larger fish prey upon. Fish will seldom eat confidently what isn't present in the natural form, so matching the hatch – observing what fly is in the air or on the water surface – is important in deciding which one of the many hundreds of flies you decide to try. Size is also relevant; selecting a fly that matches the look of hatch but is much bigger than the hatching insect, will not often work so well. Retrieving flies at a given speed is paramount to a successful outcome. Most insects move at a sedate pace, but fishing with a fry pattern fly, for example, we move quickly, in order to copy how a fry would move when being chased by a trout.

I think that fly fishermen have a blind spot about their flies. We unconsciously seem to ignore the bend of the hook and the barb it displays. We tie materials along the shank, leaving bend and barb uncovered and unadorned – except when tying a chironomid nymph, or buzzer, when we do wrap materials partly around the hook bend to imitate the hook-like nymph. In other types of fishing, the hook bend and barb are covered by worms, maggots, bread and other baits. So whatever we do to create a fly on our fly-tying vice, nymph or lure, the hook bend and barb are left naked and we grow oblivious. When we have finished tying a fly, we carefully scrutinise the shank for proportion, bulk and accuracy – we might hold the fly up by the hook bend to look at it, but does it register as part of the fly? Not to me, at least. The hook begets the fly.

Hook sizes vary considerably. International rules in competitive fly fishing state the maximum size of fly should be a 10: five-eighths of an inch from hook eye to bend of the hook, and no more than just under one inch long, including the tail that might be added. Confusingly, the larger the number allocated to the hook, the smaller the fly. I rarely use a 10 and have only a few in my fly box, as I use smaller sizes that more realistically copy the size of nymphs or emerging aquatic insects. Usually these are in a size 12 or 14, but not always. Mayfly and damselfly nymphs are much bigger mouthfuls for the trout, requiring quite a large hook to properly present a correct imitation. I have gone down to a size 24, which is very small, when fish have been smutting (taking very small flies), but that presents problems as the gape of the hook is so small that it seldom gives a good 'purchase'. If the trout takes it, you are lucky if you land one, and most of the time you don't. There are occasions, using a Daddy Longlegs or a Mayfly, when I use a much larger fly, but that is to imitate the naturals. When trout are feeding on fry – small fish which are the progeny of other fish – a larger pattern is needed to imitate them. Wet flies and mini lures are usually tied on 10s and rely on the aggressive, territorial instincts of fish to attack them. These were my flies of choice in international contests – nymphs and dry fly fishing came late to my table. Many fishermen use large flies in the form of lures, and that is perfectly OK, fly fishing is a broad church.

So we have the bare hook around which to wrap around a variety of confections in order to create a fly. One such confection is fur: seals, mole, rabbit, and hare (taken from the inside of a hare's ear – I found this gruesome when I started). Once the fur is ripped from patches of rabbit, mole and hare ear, it is dubbed onto a cotton thread – I used wax to secure this dubbing onto the hook, before realising the natural grease of your fingers would suffice – and wound around the bare hook to form the bodies of nymphs, dries and sometimes wet flies. Wet flies, still used but not so much nowadays, usually have flashier body materials to bedazzle and attract the fish's eye. They are similar to their 'mini-lure' cousins, and are attractors, moved quickly through the water to try to trigger the trout into taking them through aggression, or producing latent territorial instincts. That's the theory, anyway, although no-one can be sure.

Many theories about fishing are half-baked, or not baked at all. Some are simply confused rumours, such as the suggestion that female pheromones, transmitted somehow into the water, will encourage big fish to seek out fisherwomen, and that is why women tend to catch the record-sized fish. Some theories are more plausible, such as that high pressure helps with catch rates – more oxygen is forced into the water, which brings the fish onto the feed and makes them more active — but if air contains just 21% oxygen, not to mention the parts per million of pollutants now an (almost) normal constituent of our air, can this be so? Who knows?

Wet flies and mini lures, tied on a size 10 hook, are still favoured by competition anglers. I don't believe that they are viewed as food items, especially when they are moved so quickly, though sometimes fish will take them for small fry.

To make herls, feathers from peacock and pheasant (also used as a very effective body material), ostrich and marabou (also used as very mobile tails on lures) are spaced around the body material, and a variety of coloured wires or strong thread are tied along the shank to protect, secure and strengthen the fly. Trout have sharp teeth capable of shredding a poorly tied fly.

Hackles are tied at the front of the fly and wound around just that area to give the impression of legs and mobility as the fly moves slowly through the water. Taken from badgers and the neck feathers (capes) of poultry – chicken, partridge, guinea fowl, woodcock – and dyed to a range of colours, they can be either cock (male) or hen (female). The hen feathers are softer and more mobile, used when more movement is desired. Cul de canard (French for duck's bottom) is a delicate feather from the back of a duck, directly adjacent to its preen glands, and retains natural oils. This makes it ideal for dry flies, as it ensures buoyancy without having to be treated with waterproofing solution. Rabbit and mink are also used to tie lures, and they target trout attacking fry at the back-end of the season, in September and October. Cut into long strips, they are tied onto a long-shank hook with a tail as long again as this, whipped onto the hook. The tail's pulsating movement imparts life into the fly that trout can find irresistible, and this method can at times produce the biggest fish of the season. Flies have to be moved quickly, in long strips of the flyline. It's a young man's game for all but the shortest period, as casting becomes more intense and old muscles soon begin to ache from the effort.

Deer and elk hair can be used for bigger buoyant and dry flies. The natural materials that have been the mainstay of fly-tying for centuries also met with an explosion of new man-made materials in the twentieth and twenty-first century: Mylar, Flashabou and holographic tinsels, fritz, crystal, cactus and micro chenilles, Glo Brite flouresent flosses, glister, antron and SLF (synthetic living fibre) dubbing, and all of these in huge ranges of colours – just some of the modern materials available. I have all of these and more in my fly-tying box, and rarely use any of them. I think to myself that someday I might, but realistically, I never will. I am just a sucker for buying this bright and flashy stuff, as I suspect most fly-tyers are. In that way, we are rather similar to our prey.

At the start of our fly-tying careers we have bought the fly-tying vice and the numerous utensils needed. We first construct our flies with too much flash, too much material, and they don't look like the fly we are trying to copy, just an artist's impression (being kind). This comes about through 'just one more turn of dubbing, just another wrap of tinsel', and it is a hard lesson to learn that less is more. The first 100 flies you tie are unlikely to survive for long in your fly box – they are edged out by the better ones you eventually tie. I am an adequate fly-tyer – I have reached a certain skill set and know I won't really improve much anymore. There is a master fly-tyer called Davy McPhail, and his YouTube videos show him tying the most exquisite creations. I have tried, oh I have tried to copy them, freezing the frames as I struggle to imitate them. They are OK, but this man is so good that mine look dreadful in comparison.

Whilst the majority of my fishing experiences in this book relate to the use of flies fished in the surface film or on top of the water, most of the fish I have caught in real life have been on flies fished subsurface; flies that represent the nymph or larval versions of these surface flies. My fishing has usually occurred on lakes and reservoirs and fish feeding high in the water and are notoriously inconsistent in doing this – sometimes they are, most of the times they aren't.

Unmentioned in this book is a little fly that I have caught most of my fish on when it comes to flies fished sub-surface and if you contact the lodge of a fishing water and ask them what fly to use, what will catch there, then it's a cinch that they will mention this great little fly to you called a 'Diawl Bach'. It is a Welsh fly and translates as 'Little Devil', used as a general aquatic nymph pattern and it is deadly. Two of the most famous English fly fishermen, John Horsey and Chris Ogbourne, have advocated that sometimes it is better to have three of them on your cast – nothing else was good enough. I always have one on and it is, what I term one of my 'crutch' flies, one I turn to at times when I know no experimentation with anything else will beat what this little fly offers. The creator of the Diawl Bach is lost in the sands of time. Three welsh fishermen could claim to have been responsible for its creation but no one person has a greater claim for its invention than the others and I won't name them: I don't want to be the cause of any possible controversy that might ensue!

FLYLINE

A de rigueur fly fishing set up includes a **rod**, a **flyline** (which is spooled onto a reel), a **leader** of nylon monofilament attached to the flyline, and the **fly** attached to the end of the leader. A standard flyline is 30 meters long, crucial to propelling a fly, in the hands of a proficient caster, 20 or 25 yards accurately from boat or bank.

Early flylines were made from horsehair, which has been used, and still is, in many applications. Ancient Egyptians made horsehair wigs. In the sixteenth century, people wore it to deter lice, and in the eighteenth century horsehair wigs appeared in courtrooms, where they can still be seen today. Brushes for hair, shaving, teeth and shoes were made from horsehair, and in the early 1900s it was used as a suture material by surgeons performing facelifts. In upholstery, horsehair is resilient and not prone to compression-forming lumps; it doesn't clump together. Textiles, pottery and even jewellery have been made from the stuff. Today, 150-200 strands are used to create bows for violins, violas, cellos and double bass, as horsehair is credited with bringing a sweeter sound to the instrument.

Flylines were originally made from the long hairs of a white stallion or gelding, as mares would urinate on their tails, weakening the hairs. By braiding long lengths it was possible to create the first flylines. By the eighteenth century, the many tiny knots necessary along the braided flyline were largely eliminated, as mechanisation in textile manufacturing meant that horsehair could be woven in an almost knotless line. In the nineteenth century, horsehair was replaced by silk, an amazing material first used between 4000–3000 BC, its history and usage would merit a book of its own. Still, it didn't become popular as a flyline until the 1860s, when lines became thinner, less prone to water logging, and easier to cast. They sank (but so did horsehair lines), and new techniques required a floating line, so large quantities of lanolin was smeared along their lengths. Silk lines have largely been replaced by modern PVC lines, but some are still made and used by owners of split cane rods. Now antiques themselves, silk flylines do have the bonus of not coiling in cold weather as PVC ones tend to do, and they are lighter so cause less disturbance when the fly lands and lifts off from the water. They still need a floatant, usually a silicone, applied along their length.

Today's flylines have a PVC coating with a braided nylon core. The coating is smooth, to enable a near-frictionless passage through the rod rings when casting. Flylines come in all sorts of colours — magenta pink, green, blue, white, grey and yellow — and for many different applications. Some sink slowly, others fast; some hover just below the surface water; some sink at a uniform rate, whilst others sink belly first, so that the fly descends and then comes back up in a U-shaped curve. This type used to be the only sinking flyline you could buy before modern flyline development, but recently it has been reintroduced and sold as a new 'concept' in sunk line techniques. There's always some enterprising soul in the marketing department of fishing tackle manufacturers who takes advantage of the chimp-like DNA present in all fishermen when it comes to the latest tackle. I have fifteen different flylines, all doing different jobs, but I mostly use floating flylines, as these days I fish the top of the water for trout swimming in the upper layers. I also go for the more somber colours of grey or light green, to minimise any flash coming from the line that might alert my quarry. Flylines and fly rods are matched by the weight of the flyline. A 6-weight line loaded onto an 8-weight rod is insufficient to work the rod when casting, as the stiffer rod will not flex enough to power the line. A 7-weight rod would function, just, but is hard work. Rods have to be matched to the correct flyline to achieve distance between you and the fish.

Flylines have come a long way since the horsehair lines of the sixteenth century. Modern flylines are quite durable, which is just as well when their average price is around £50. When I first started boat fishing I was inept enough to damage a few flylines beyond repair after they accidentally came in contact with the propellor. It is an easy thing to do. You might be looking at the scenery or attending to your tackle, maybe tying on another fly, and your flyline is floating on the water when your partner starts the motor. In seconds the line is wrapped around the propeller, which you then have to raise in order to release the irretrievably damaged flyline. You soon learn to pay attention when your partner suggests a move, it is too expensive a lesson to ignore!

RODS

Rods, like flylines, have come an awfully long way. Stone inscriptions from ancient Egypt, China, Greece and Rome, dating back to 2000 BC show fishing rods, albeit as just simple sticks or poles. Our knowledge of rod evolution begins in the fifteenth century, when rods became more distinguishable from a stick, and sections made of various woods were combined. The 'butt section', which is held, and to which a reel would later be fitted, was the stiffest part, yielding to a middle section of more flexible wood. A third, even more flexible section allowed the line to be propelled through the air in a whip-lash action. These were joined together by a small metal bracelet, or ferrule. The butt section was made from maple wood, while the middle section was fashioned from hickory, ash or willow. The tip made of hazel accomplished, insofar as it was possible, a through-actioned rod that could cast a flyline and subdue fish as strong as a salmon. Modern rods still follow this fundamental principle, but have been engineered to produce more of a 'through'-action rod, meaning that when playing a fish, the curvature is effortlessly distributed along the length of the rod.

Most early rods were made by fishermen or fisherwomen themselves, as there were few tackle shops. By the seventeenth century this had changed. Few anglers made their own rods, and rods had become more specialised. Before this, the same rod would be used for fly fishing, bait fishing or trolling, but now there were specialised rods for catching trout and salmon. In the seventeenth and eighteenth century, baleen, a type of whalebone harvested from the blue, minke and humpback whales began to be used for the tips of rods. Baleen, also used for corset stays and umbrella ribs, came from the whale's upper jaw, which is comb-like as they have no need of teeth, being filter feeders. In the mid-1800s rod makers began to use bamboo (which wasn't entirely new as it had previously been used as a tip section), which did away with all other wooden materials. Rod makers split the bamboo into six strips, then glued them together to create a hexagonal shape which transformed the performance of the fly rod; it was lighter, more responsive when playing a fish, and the 'action' of the rod threw a fly-line further. The split cane rod had arrived, and remained superior to every rod produced for over 100 years. Even today, it has its dedicated aficionados.

After the First World War, the introduction of fibreglass rods ended the dominance of split cane, but this dominance too was not to last. In the late 1960s a new material, carbon fibre, saw off both fibre-glass and split cane rods (though as I have said, some anglers still use them). Developed by the Royal Aircraft Establishment at Farnborough, and introduced into rod making, carbon fibre is strong and lightweight, and allows rod tapers to be engineered to produce a variety of different 'actioned' rods. Carbon fibre rods now account for most fly rod sales.

Rods sometimes prove unsatisfactory to fly fishermen who have spent several hundred pounds only to find that the rod just doesn't cut the mustard: rods must match your temperament and fishing ability. A good rod to one is a bad rod for another. They are very personal, though it's hard to explain why. When you fish with the right rod, you meld with it, and when you break it, that is a disaster – you feel like you have broken your right arm! A modern fly rod is a wonderful creation, light but strong, and almost indestructible when used as it's meant to be used. Still, on some occasions – such as when I let my ten-year-old accident-prone grandson run through some trees with the rod held upright – it is possible to break it beyond repair. That rod was one of my favourites, fifteen years old, and I couldn't buy another one. It had been discontinued, and the makers had replaced it with a so-called superior rod. I bought the replacement and it just wasn't as good, and was quite a bit more expensive too. Manufacturers seem to have reached a point in the evolution and the technology of rod making where they can't improve the rod any more.

Another material might replace carbon fibre in rod manufactur-ing eventually; boron has been tried with some success, but discarded because of its high cost in comparison to carbon fibre. In my opin-ion, unless a new revolutionary material arrives (I don't know, maybe graphene might one day be that material) there is no room for improvement with carbon fibre – makers may tinker around with it but its full potential, I think, has been reached. But rod manufacturers and tackle shops need to survive, and rods are an important source of revenue, so super-duper rods, increasingly expensive (some reach as much as £1,300) are marketed as better than last year's model – claims that are, really, nonsense. This occurs year in and year out – this year's model is better than last year's, they insist, and the poor beleaguered fishermen who open the latest tackle brochures wonder whether a new rod might be the answer to increasing their catch rate. All fishermen desire new tackle, and well, they are hooked! But a new rod won't make you catch any more fish than you would or wouldn't catch anyway. The rod is important, but fishing successfully isn't down to your rod.

| 1 |

River Test in Hampshire

Parachute Adams

The Chalkstream River Test in Hampshire is a place of pilgrimage for fly fishers the world over. This wonderful, meandering, narrow, shallow, crystal-clear river 'test' was where, in the nineteenth century, dry fly fishing developed, then spread throughout the world. River Test 'beats' – a section of bankside that is available to fish from – can be very expensive, with day tickets costing hundreds of pounds for peak season fishing when the Mayfly hatches occur. I am not able to spend that amount of money on a single day's fishing, so I fish for grayling at a fraction of the cost of the Spring and Summer trout fishing. It is sad that for a long time the riverkeepers considered grayling vermin and wanted them removed to give the brown trout unimpeded access to the river's larder. Riverkeepers, guardians of these exclusive waters, carry out the orders of the riparian owners, their employers, whose interest is in maintaining trout fishing, a valuable source of income generated by the paying fishermen. They often regard fish other than brown trout as unwelcome competitors for the aquatic life that nourishes and sustains the trout. At times I have arrived at a lunchtime destination to discover dozens of grayling lying dead on the bank, after fellow anglers heeded the riverkeepers' instructions and killed all that they caught. I will only kill a fish for food. Fortunately, attitudes have begun to change and grayling are now returned. Hopefully this policy will continue. Abstraction and pollution have taken a toll on the aquatic life of even a pristine river such as the Test. There is just less food now for all fish to eat, and so the pressure is on for the grayling, and they may or may not be culled depending on their population within the various beats.

I have been lucky enough to fish this river for grayling at the close season for brown trout, with no sure bet what fish would take a fly – both eat the same food, so it is just as likely that a trout will snaffle the fly as a grayling. Spring and summer fly hatches had long gone, but a few flies were still ing when I fished the Longparish beat in early November. The wind wasn't strong but was enough to dislodge the leaves from the trees, sending them fluttering down to rest on the riverbank and river. I arrived at the top of the beat with about 80 yards to fish a stretch of wide, slow-moving water. Tucked close into the far bank, wading as silently as I could, I cast a dry fly to the grayling I could spot, or to their rises. Because the water is crystal clear and shallow, it is a given that the fish will be aware of you. It is best to spend a little time sitting immobile on the bank, as this seems to allow the fish to accept your presence, before carefully wading out into the water. It takes self-control though, because spotting fish or their 'rises' – when they rise to take surface flies – usually galvanizes one into premature action. On this early November day, I was fishing a size 14 dry fly called a Parachute Adam, or Para-Adams which didn't sit on top of the water, but in the surface film, and was more readily seen due to an upright wing of white wool, a great visual asset standing out amongst the numerous leaves that had been shed this Autumn, now on their way downstream.

The Adams fly, of which I was fishing a variant, was borne out of an angler's failed fishing experience. Charles F. Adams was an attorney from Ohio, fishing the Boardman River on a summer's day in 1922, casting to numerous trout who refused all that he offered them. Having failed to 'match the' and mimic the flies that were on the river that day, he noted what fly had been most prominent, and described it to his old friend and fishing companion, Leonard Halladay. Halladay tied up a fly, and the first time Charles Adams used it he had one of those golden days that are all so rare when catching trout. Len Halladay named the fly the Adams after his friend.

I edged my way slowly upstream, hooking the leaves that floated downstream, as well as the grayling, that were feeding well. There is no doubt that the number of fish that I caught were superfluous to the experience of fishing on as near a perfect day as it could be. It was not the number of grayling that I hooked that mattered most (I had had better catches), it was just participating in what was an ineffable experience. I did not even need to change my fly; sometimes I end the day completely baffled at how I could have used the number of flies that have disrupted the tidy, methodical rows of flies of my fly box.

I have rarely seen another's fly box that isn't immaculate before the fishing starts. We may be very messy with our personal effects, but nothing is as neat and tidy as our fly boxes. They are a very personal thing. I have known anglers with just one huge box maybe containing 400+ flies. These boxes were usually made of balsa wood, appropriated from tobacconists where they once displayed dozens of cigars, then lined with high-density foam. However, the constant re-moval and re-insertion of the hook's sharp barbs soon destroyed the foam, and the flies would flop any which way, so the box soon became useless. Smaller boxes became more popular, as it wasn't easy secreting large boxes into your fishing vest when mobility was necessary to fish. These smaller, plastic boxes, the size of an old cigarette case but double the depth, came lined with a rigid rubber insert, and the flies gripped at the bend of the hook, so the sharp hook point had no contact and did little damage. I've known fishermen to have a dozen smaller boxes – I have around seven, containing more than 400 flies. I once knew a brave angler who was determined to prune his fly collection to just six types, but it was a battle lost, as new patterns are created and variants of existing patterns made almost on a daily basis. It messed with his head, and subsequently his resolve.

Fly boxes have to accommodate a lot of flies. I don't think it is possible to know how many different fly patterns have been invented in the 500 or so years of fly fishing – my guess was maybe 300-400 – and I was surprised to discover that I was way out: several sources suggest there are several thousand different flies, and I think they must be right. Flies are tied for many different species, and although they may not always be like the nymphs, lures, dry and wet flies of the trout fisherman, their categorisation would still be that of a 'fly'. A successful fly pattern will then have been modified into a variant of the original, where fly-tyers have added and subtracted different materials: fur, tinsels, feathers, fluorescent wools, threads, chenilles, herls and beads. A famous pattern can sometimes spawn eight or so variants on the original. Sometimes for instance, a ribbing on a fly is changed from fine wire to a holographic tinsel, or a small bright fluorescent wool collar is included at its head. Bewilderingly for the layman, you have then to tie these in various hook sizes from size 16 (small) to size 8 (large), then there are the long shank hooks and so on. I only possess flies in three sizes, but if you have one pattern in a size 14 then you must have at least two, and usually four, as flies are lost or damaged regularly, then multiply this by the three sizes I keep – I now have 12 flies tied in one pattern. Then on top of that you have the popular variants of that pattern tied up. Our spouses do not know why we spend so many hours at the fly-tyers bench!

From our fly box we have to pick one to tie onto our leader. With this choice comes confusion and indecision, created by the many confections that we have created. But then it seems to me comparisons, judgments, must be made constantly by all of us as part of decision-making, almost part of our DNA. The important Indian Philosopher Jiddu Khristnamurti, in his book *Freedom from the Known*, relates how the use of comparisons can be divisive and counterproductive for all of us: "We think in comparisons – deep and shallow, happy and unhappy. We are always measuring, comparing". It seems to me that we all compare, and at the basic level, when we compare rich with poor and acknowledge that as being unjust, it is a valid comparison, producing a realisation that wealth should be more equally distributed. However, it is unfortunate that comparing race, creed or religion often leads to prejudice and disharmony.

Jiddu Khristnamurti was born in India in 1895. His father, Jiddu Narayaniah, was employed as an Official of the British Colonial Administration, but gained employment as a clerk at the headquarters of the Theosophical Society in Madras. When Khristnamurti was fourteen, he came to the attention of Charles Webster Leadbetter, a leading figure in the Theosophical Society, who believed Khristnamurti to possess spiritual and mystical qualities. Leadbetter started to nurture the adolescent Jiddu, becoming convinced that the boy would become a spiritual leader and a likely vehicle for the Lord Maitreya; a spiritual entity supposed to periodically appear on earth as a world teacher to guide human evolution. The Theosophical Society created 'The Order of the Star in the East' in preparation for the expected appearance of the world leader, and Khristnamurti was named as its head. However, in 1929, Khristnamurti dissolved the Order of the Star of the East, stating "I maintain that Truth is a pathless land and you cannot approach it by any path whatsoever, by any religion, by any sect. The moment you follow someone you cease to follow the truth". Throughout the remainder of his life, he disavowed all organisational structures.

Like everyone, I have made bad decisions based on comparisons, from the choice of what fly to tie onto my flyline (inconsequential, perhaps) to an investment decision that hit my pocket (and landed a blow to my self-esteem), but it was comparing yourself to others that Khristnamurti eschewed. If I measure myself against another who is more intelligent, brighter, more outgoing, considerate, then feelings of inferiority can ensue. If I didn't compare, how would I have come to that conclusion? If I now try to be more like the person I am comparing myself with, then I am denying what I am myself. In the process of not comparing, I accept others completely as who they are. So Kristnamurti, I think, believed that in order to discover who we really are, we have to unshackle ourselves from the untruths that feed pain, pleasure and fear through unrealistic and harmful misunderstandings that come about when measuring oneself against another. Is growth really driven by comparison? Khristnamurti would consider human and personal insightfulness, knowledge of oneself, the ultimate growth.

It might seem odd, but most fishermen, even those I have known for as long as twenty years, are a mystery to me. When we meet, we talk about fishing, then we fish and afterwards say our goodbyes, with no interaction of a personal nature. I might know what their job is, what type of fishermen they are – dry fly or nymph man, accomplished or otherwise – and sometimes I learn a little about their personal lives. But whether they are married, have children, are gay or straight, usually remains unknown to me. The anonymity that we all exhibit when it comes to our personal and private life is simply, surely, because we become fishermen to leave behind or to untether from our other lives. The absence of knowing others on a personal level creates an absence of judgment or comparison, tenets of the philosophy that Kristnamurti preached. Adrenaline surges that keep us hooked to this sport weren't the reason we took it up – after all, that came later, when we started to catch a few fish. I have fished with all kinds of people – men, mostly – from millionaires to paupers. I have travelled the world with some, had pints and meals with others, but only established a personal relationship with a few. Of course, why would you make a personal relationship? You are there for the fishing, not social interaction. We are fishermen, some better than others, but nevertheless, just fishermen. The upside is that I have learnt a lot, about all aspects of our sport, from some very good fishermen – world-class fishermen – willing to share, within the confines of a relationship based on fly fishing, all of their experiences and knowledge.

Lunchtime on this day on the Test, we are convivial – pleased with the morning's sport, sipping glasses of red wine and eating barbequed food for lunch, and we talk about the morning's fishing or about another fishing occasion some of us might have shared, that is as far as it goes. We are, this lunchtime, at a ted wooden building of nineteenth century origin about three times the size of a garden shed, with wooden benches running down two sides of it. Directly by the side of it runs the main river and what is called the Hatch Pool. I have never discovered whether its name derives from hatches of flies, that are more prevalent here, or because the water at this point seems to go underneath the side of the wooden structure through a sort of hatch. I know, although no-one was fishing there yet, someone soon would – my fisherman friends all know it can produce, at times, a lot of fish. Mumbling about trying my luck, I wander off.

Autumn leaves are slippery underfoot as I walk along the bank. I arrive at the entry point, 40 yards or so from where the river deepens and descends through the hatch, the water barely covering the boots of my waders. I cross over the river to the other side where there are fewer trees that might impede and interrupt my backcasts. A slow movement forward and to the left and the river starts to deepen. Where it is deepest, at the hatch, is where the fish lie. I have on my line a weighted nymph called a Copper John, the body of which is copper wire, with a tungsten bead head, designed to sink quickly; ideal in fast running water. John Barr of Boulder, Colorado first invented this fly in 1993, but he developed it over the next three years and it represents a wide range of larvae, pupae and nymphs. This is a single fly set-up. I have a 9' monofilament nylon leader connected to my flyline. I have looped onto the leader 5' from the Copper John a white tuft of wool previously saturated in floatant which will act as a float. I am prepared to strike at the slightest twitch it displays, for this isn't visual fishing – you don't see a fish take your fly, you just react to any movement of the white wool. This is the only possible method if you want to be successful in a deep pool, but there is just a small area where the fish congregate, and just after three metres the pool shallows up and the fish do not venture into these shallows. So I cast, wait and watch, cast wait and watch, and each of these sequences may only last for 30 seconds a time.

Casting now into the deepest part, the fly sinks and when it is at its deepest (only experience can tell you when this is), raising the rod slightly will propel the fly in an upward curve through the water, which seems to compel a grayling or trout to 'eat' this intruder. A further upward motion with the rod 'sets' the hook, and you are in business. Truthfully, I'm never as successful as some of my fellow fly fishermen fishing the Hatch Pool, and today is no exception, but I have caught a grayling that might have gone 2lbs – the biggest of the day for me. My little river rod did well to tame it as it careened around the river, and I thought that it might be something special. It wasn't, but it was a good fish, and I was relieved and just a little disappointed when it came to the net. Fishing the deep weighted nymph isn't one of my strengths when it comes to fly fishing methodology, but few are expert in every aspect of this sport. I'm OK with that – we are fishermen all, with varying skill sets.

The fly hatches have now vanished, so fishing the dry fly isn't so productive, but I am grateful to carry on with this method until the light starts to fade. November mist shrouds the river, and it is time for the long journey home.

| 2 |

Float tubing in New Zealand

Buzzer

Lake Otamangakau, Lake O to the locals, is situated on the North Island of New Zealand, within Tongariro National Park, twenty minutes from Turangi, and Mount Tongariro in the background. We were there in February to fish its crystal-clear water for large rainbow and brown trout. We had chosen to fish from a 'float tube', a first for me.

Float tubing originated in the US. I am told that originally it involved using an inflated inner tube from a lorry tyre within which a sort of seat was suspended where you could sit, with legs dangling down and flippers on your feet to power forward or backward motion. The fishing tackle industry soon realised its potential, and sleek, commercial models came to market. It is, to me, a universal truth that all fishermen are extremely gullible where fishing tackle is concerned. Quite a few bought float tubes (myself included) only to discover that their use was limited: many waters simply wouldn't allow you to use them, citing health and safety or high insurance premiums they weren't prepared to pay. This meant they were useless, and dangerous too when there was a wind, as you could be blown somewhere you didn't want to be, lose control and be unable to exit the water. Today, however, we had picked a perfect Summer's day with little wind. Aware of much laughter from the bystanders on the bank, I had to enter the water from the shallows, walking backwards because of the flippers, with what appeared to be a giant tutu around my waist. Float tubing gives its user a low surface profile, so it's possible to get very close to trout feeding on the surface. That day there was little surface activity and only a few flies on the water, though on our travel from Turangi the roadside bushes and trees had reverberated with the sound of millions of cicadas – they hadn't reached Lake O.

Float tubing is a marvelous fishing method, though it is time-consuming to inflate the bladders necessary for its construction, having retrieved it from all the other fishing gear crammed into the car. With all your other fishing paraphernalia, but just one rod, you walk it down to the water's edge, stumbling on the rough terrain, the tube on your back, looking not unlike a ninja turtle. All this can take the better part of an hour of precious fishing time, but that is quickly forgotten once afloat. You have entered a sensual world, neither wholly in the water like a swimmer, nor on top of the water like a kayaker, but with the latter's perspective of the water and its surroundings. Weightless, suspended, there is a pleasure in just working the fins with your legs and moving effortlessly along. I did so and moved slowly out to midwater. I had two flies tied to my leader, both imitating the pupae of an aquatic insect of the chironomid family, a non-biting midge colloquially called 'buzzers' due to the sound the adult emits once hatched from the water.

My fly was invented by Dr Howard Bell, the inventor of a number flies still in use nearly 100 years after he created them. At a time when flashy 'attractor' patterns were the norm, Dr Bell employed the alternative tactic of using artificial flies that represented the shape and form of the aquatic insects present in Blagdon Lake, where he fished regularly. Bell was born near Reigate in 1888 and became a General Practitioner after studying at Cambridge, and then St Bartholomew's Hospital, in London. Although he was quite a shy and reclusive man, Bell and his wife were well known in Blagdon village where they lived. Mrs. Bell was kind, but autocratic, and the consultant that visited Howard Bell when he became seriously ill towards the end of his life was the first person to discover that she was the daughter of a Scottish Earl, brought up in a castle, and taught by a governess. She ran away to become a nurse, against her father's orders, and served in World War One as a volunteer nurse. According to her, the family's fortune was lost when her brother ran away with a Frenchwoman, but she still managed to leave over a million pounds in her will – most of which, on her death, benefited cat and dog homes. Although she didn't fish, she accompanied him every year to Scotland where he fished the River Spey for salmon.

The Bells were by no means poor: they had a large staff for just the two of them, but Howard Bell eschewed all prospects of obtaining the fame of other famous fly inventors, because he never published any articles on his methods or flies – he wanted a quiet, uninterrupted life. There are only three photos of him in existence – all of them appear with him in his Home Guard Uniform from the Second World War. He could be forthright, at times, and would not suffer fools gladly. Dr Trick, the doctor who took over Bell's surgery on his retirement, tells of several instances when Dr Bell walked into Dr Trick's surgery and, if it was crowded, relieved Dr Trick's workload by pointing to several individuals shouting "You, you and you, there's nothing wrong with you, come back another time!"

Bell served in the First World War with the Royal Army Medical Corps and was a survivor of the third battle of Ypres. I always imagine that it was the horrors of his wartime experiences tending the wounded and dying in Flanders that motivated him to take up the gentle art of fly fishing and lead a quiet life in idyllic surroundings. There have been times when I have needed fishing as a distraction from an every-day life event but, God knows, nothing can come close to this man's experiences (for which I am thankful). I think I understand the succour that fishing Blagdon would have given him from the memories of the nightmarish events that he and so many of his generation had to endure. He died in 1974, aged eighty-six, and is a seminal influence on modern still water fly fishing.

My visit to Lake O and Mount Tongariro was over twenty years ago, and my memories of their physical characteristics have faded, however I remember a barren and isolated beauty, created as a result of the Tongariro hydropower scheme. It was one of the venues for the world fly fishing championships in 2008. Mount Tongariro is the northernmost of three active volcanos on the central north island, the last eruption of which was in 2012, the first since 1897. Though there were no fatalities, the ash and the smell of sulphur were reported as far away as Napier and Hastings. The Tongariro national park is a UNESCO world heritage site, and the mountain summits are of great religious significance to the local Maori people. It is a major draw for people attempting the Tongariro alpine crossing, one of the world's best one-day hikes. The snows in winter help showcase its exceptional beauty.

The two buzzer flies I have opted for on a fifteen-foot nylon leader have differing qualities: the point fly, tied at the end of my leader, is an olive buzzer pattern tied on a heavyweight hook and slim, so entering the water it sinks quickly; a smaller black buzzer on a lightweight hook is attached to a six-inch length of nylon running perpendicular to the main leader, some five feet from the heavy point fly. These buzzer (chironomid) flies are found in lakes throughout the world. We find them back home in the UK and here in New Zealand. Wherever they proliferate, fish will eat them. Fishing with artificial imitations of them can be very productive.

Once I have cast the flies out, they sink quickly, and the 15 foot leader is now vertical in the water. I watch the tip of my flyline for any twitches that might register an interest in my sunk flies. I fish these flies by slowly, very slowly, retrieving the flyline. You can't fish them too slowly (I know anglers that are very successful by not retrieving them at all) but you can fish them too fast. My flies imitate the pupae of aquatic insects as they move towards the surface to hatch. They move in small, jerky movements just a few inches at a time, and they are picked off easily by trout and other fish. The sheer number of these pupae ensure that many make it to the surface and the next stage of their life cycle. Fishing these flies, I am ready both for a gentle 'take' by a trout, or sometimes an explosive one so violent that it results in a 'smash take', where the fish breaks the fly from the leader and the trout swims away to freedom.

Around Lake O there are four fly fishermen in float tubes. Two of them have rods bending and are into fish, then suddenly it is my turn, as my rod jerks downwards. I don't need to set the hook, as the trout has done that by aggressively taking the fly. Trout on Lake O are large, growing sometimes to four kilos, and with full fins and wide tails, they are fit enough to pull yards of flyline off your reel as the fish heads for the horizon. It is a heart-stopping, adrenaline-filled moment as you wait to see whether the fish remains hooked: it could easily straighten the hook, throw the hook off, or break the 5lb breaking-strain nylon.

I have a fish on and in the middle of the lake there are no boundaries to inhibit this fish as it dives one way then another. I cannot allow it to react as it wants to, and have to apply 'rod pressure' so there is a strength-sapping bend in the rod – but not too much – too much can court disaster and although rods hardly ever break whilst playing a fish, it does happen. The fish isn't giving up easily and within 30 seconds of hooking a fish, experience dictates how to proceed, as no two fish will have the same reactions. I decide to tire it and not bully it into the net, and it runs. Then I think perhaps more pressure would be better?

I am always aware of self-doubt when I am playing a fish. You banish that, you can only do your best. This time, it is OK – as the fish tires, I gather up the line it tore off from my reel and slowly apply the pressure that brings it nearer to me and my net. This fish is around two kilos and is a superb specimen; well-formed fins, wide tail and the iridescent colouring of a rainbow trout.

There are times when I am but a primeval being, a cave man. Ancient instincts flood through me when I hook a fish, adrenaline surges through my veins, and the latent hunting instinct of prehistoric man takes over. I can't help it – I might be absorbed in the beauty of my surroundings, at peace, then I am high on the 'fix' of adrenaline supplied when a fish takes my fly. Although the high lessens as I coax the fish to the net, it is there. I think that, although others might deny it, this is one of the reasons why we fish. However sophisticated you think you may be, our prehistoric genes don't care.

I slide the fish carefully back into the water, content for the moment to take in the vista of Mount Tongariro's barren beauty. Fly fishing can engender a reflective nature in some of us, and there are times when I am fishing that I enter quite a meditative state of mind – though mind and body have to be aligned. Even then, it cannot be as intense as a guided meditation, something I experienced myself five years ago. The guided mediation course was called Vipassana, and it was brought to the West by Satya Narayan Goenka, who remains one of the most important teachers of meditation of the last century. He addressed the United Nations General Assembly at the Millennium World Peace Summit of Religious and Spiritual leaders in August 2000, and was present at the World Economic Forum in Davos that same year. Vipassana was practised twenty-five centuries ago by Gotama the Buddha. After five hundred years, it disappeared from India, but was maintained by a continuous stream of Vipassana teachers in Myanmar (then called Burma) until the present day. U Ba Knin, a student of Saya Thetgyi, who was himself a student of the venerable Ledi Sayadaw, popularised the technique and instructed others, including Goenka, in the practice. The earliest modern writer of Vipassana manuals was a Burmese monk named Medawi (1728 – 1816), who was influential in reviving the Burmese interest in meditation practices. Although it was a by-product of Buddhism, Goenka taught Vipassana meditation as a technique to be learnt, emphasising that there would be no religious overtones that might restrict people from going on a retreat. By doing this, he opened it up to all.

I became interested in Vipassana meditation due to health problems that weren't responding well to medical treatment. Concidentally, I first came to an awareness of Vipassana through the writer Tim Parks, who detailed his experiences of the meditation in his autobiographical book *Teach Us to Sit Still*, having had the same health issues as myself.

Can a reader have a relationship with an author? It cannot be reciprocal, but I felt I had this with Tim Parks, although he is certainly unaware of me. I have read several of his books, including *Teach Us to Sit Still*, which, to me, was a revelation. We shared a similar condition relating to our prostrates, which meant they squeezed against the urethra, creating hesitancy in the flow of urine. Before I came across *Teach Us to Sit Still*, I had had two TURPS operations to reduce the size of my prostate which hadn't helped much. I was intrigued that Tim Parks had avoided this so-called 'gold standard' medical procedure in favour of more holistic approaches. After trying several of these, he opted for a Vipassana meditation course. What did that accomplish? He writes that the major benefit was recreating a connection with his body that had somehow been lost. It is easy, if your world resides solely in your head, to pay no attention to, and therefore have little relationship with, your physical body. In Vipassana meditation, the whole meditation revolves around the body, so it was no surprise that I experienced this reconnection as well. It begets an understanding of the body that you possess, enabling you to reconcile with your physical frailties. Whilst making the condition no better, it reduces one's natural resistance against it, and engenders an acceptance instead. Vipassana is a practice I still carry out today.

Satya Narayana Goenka was born in 1924 in Burma to Indian parents. He grew up in a conservative Hindu family that fled to India when the Japanese invaded Burma in 1942. Upon their return home, he led the family-run conglomerate of businesses that included exports, textiles and agriculture. At thirty, he was elected Head of the Rangoon Chamber of Commerce. Around this time he began to experience intense migraine headaches. Taking the advice of a friend, he sought out a meditation teacher, U Ba Knin, under whom he would study for fourteen years.

In 1969, Goenka relinquished all business connections, moved to India and began teaching Vipassana meditation full time. He did not teach monks and nuns, the usual students in meditation, instead accepting any student, regardless of caste or gender. The technique of Vipassana is secular, allied to no religion or belief system; it is open to people of all faiths or none. 1976 saw the opening of his first meditation centre in Igatpuri. Six years later, he started to train assistant teachers, now numbering over 1300. From the beginning, he taught ten-day intensive meditation retreats, and today, Vipassana courses taught in the tradition of his teacher, U Ba Knin are held in 310 locations in 94 countries. There are about 176 permanent Vipassana meditation centres worldwide and as many as 120,000 people are thought to attend courses yearly.

The organisation of the meditation centres is decentralized and self-sufficient. Goenka did not want the whole network to become a sectarian religion or cult, and in this, he has succeeded: courses have even been held in prisons in India and America. Supported by voluntary donations made at the end of the course by people who want to contribute to future courses, previous students are recruited to cook, clean and perform other general duties when a course is in progress, so there is no charge for the guidance, lodgings or food. Your course has already been paid by another person and if you can afford to, you should pay to facilitate another's.

I remember arriving at the meditation centre near Hereford on a raw spring day. Our phones and all electronic devices were locked away as all outside contact was banned – nothing was allowed at all. We had to practice complete silence for the ten days of the course. Even visual contact such as nodding to another person was not allowed. Our only verbal communication took place every three days or so, when the leaders of the course selected four or five people to ask them individually how they were coping with the stringent regime of daily twelve-hour meditation sessions. The sessions were staged throughout the day, starting at 6am, following the sound of a gong at 5.30am. The food, two meals a day, was good: vegetarian, of course, but nutritious and served up in a large room, split along its length by a wall which segregated the men from women. This seemed a bit pointless, as we were all supposed to be incommunicado anyway and no one would have the opportunity to meet until the course was completed. The meditation hall was a large room in another building and, in use, men were positioned on the left with women to the right. Most sat in the lotus position on large cushions with brown blankets wrapped around them in the chilly hall. I had obtained a kitchen chair, as I was recovering from a bout of sciatica. Roughly 150 students, with an equal number of males and females, were on my course. Goenka would address us in a mellifluous voice via a big screen at the end of each day's session, about interpreting our day's meditation.

There is an unequalled and wonderful sense of peace and tranquility when you are in the meditation hall, being part of a body of 150 others who, let's face it, have to be of a similar nature to you. I had never experienced such an atmosphere before. In attending you are selfish, of course, as it is, after all, about you, but you are also unselfish in not wanting to distract from the experiences of others. I was uncomfortable in being unable to suppress a cough, a fallout from a recent cold. It sounded like a thunderclap in the silence. Away to my left, a woman's cough seemed to echo mine. I learnt to time my cough so when she coughed, so did I, and I think she did the same as well. As the days went by, it became less of an issue, and it didn't seem to matter in the end. Mealtimes were held in silence, and everybody, with slow deliberation, ate with relish. There was an air of serenity present. One felt unusually happy to be amongst the human race again, with people whose faces exhibited such calmness and dignity. Buddhists call this the 'noble silence', an apt name.

On the third day, whilst in my room, I heard some raised, un-happy voices. I later learnt from a server (a previous student who had volunteered to do the catering and cleaning) that two men had left the course – they hadn't expected it to be so hardcore, and maybe, also, Western expectations played a part. We are all taught that to do some-thing is to try to attain, achieve and gain 'something' from the activity, and expectations in our society are a reflection of that mindset. Our Western civilisation focusses on goals, and cultivates and reinforces the idea that in undertaking something, one should be rewarded. Not one part of this mindset is valid when it comes to Vipassana. It is a paradox, but entering a Vipassana session with the view of gaining or achieving something will produce nothing but frustration.

My server friend told me that more men drop out than women, and in his opinion, women were tougher and able to cope more. I didn't agree with him. There are perceptual differences inbred in the two sexes – men are expected to be oriented towards achievement more than women – and as such, they are less likely to accept what is put before them in a ten-day Vipassana course. Although we all receive prior information from the course managers, if this doesn't fit with their expectations, they are more likely to quit. To me, the way men and women physically interact with their bodies helps women commit and develop coping strategies that mean they are more likely to complete the course. Male bodies are not affected by menstruation or pregnancy, so men often do not have the personal relationship with their bodies, and with discomfort, that nature demands of women. I think this confounds some men, who have to connect with their body in a way that, until that point, has been alien to them.

It is a bone of contention amongst some men that a lot of record-sized fish have been caught by women, when statistically they simply shouldn't have. After all, they argue, women anglers are not that common. Some crazy reasons have been expostulated as to why, and it has even been suggested that pheromones emitted by the fairer sex tempt the fish to them. These theories are put forward by, I might add, desperate men unconvinced that woman could possess the necessary skills. A record salmon was caught by a Ghillie's daughter, Georgina Ballantine in 1922. It came from the River Tay and weighed 64lbs. Annalisa Barbieri writes in an article when she was fishing correspondent for the *Independent*, that Georgina's feat wasn't unusual: in March 1923, Doreen Davey's 59lb salmon was caught on the River Wye, the biggest spring salmon ever caught, and Clementina Morison in October 1924 caught a 61lb salmon on a fly from the River Deveron. In September 1927, Gladys Blanche took four hours to land a 55lb salmon which came from the River Awe, and in the Autumn of 1928, Lettice Ward caught a 50lb one on the River Tay. It is not surprising that men believe this anthropomorphic nonsense about pheromones, as it would let men off the hook – some men tie salmon flies which incorporate female pubic hair, presumably from their wives or girlfriends. I do remember, I was fishing a competition once and had drawn a woman as a boat partner. I ended up with five fish, she had four, and beat me on weight. The fact is that women more commonly have what most men lack: patience.

Patience is a somewhat misleading term for those practicing Vipassana meditation, because being patient implies that there is an expectation that something is going to happen, and that it's just a case of waiting, of being patient. In fact, is better to accept that something might or might not happen and be satisfied with both these outcomes. Patience and expectation seem to be inextricably entwined, when in fact it is not about waiting, but about accepting the present and the future, whatever it might provide. Sometimes after a session of Vipassana meditation you conclude 'Well, that was a waste of time', because you approached it with an expectation of something – maybe you wanted to feel at peace with everything, or realise some revelation that solved a problem, but it doesn't work that way, at least for me. In the early days I would end a session with this disappointment, but many sessions later it didn't matter anymore. After a session when nothing much had happened, I would still look forward to the next one, and as I go about my fishing now, this non-expectation has freed me from the 'must catch at all costs' attitude. I can just enjoy the process, the moment.

Courses start with the observation of the natural breath, a practice called Anapana. This concentration prepares one for the Vipassana practice itself, which involves observing bodily sensations with equanimity, and with the awareness of the interconnection between mind and body. After the first three days practicing Anapana meditation, Vipassana meditation commences with the observation of bodily sensations: you focus on the crown of your head and follow a systematic and conscious movement through all parts of your body, finishing at the feet, and then reverse the process. Goenka described these bodily sensations as the result of sub-atomic activity in the body. Sensations occur as you proceed to examine every part of your body, and they can be both pleasant and painful. Goenka, in his talks about not attaching to sensations as they arise, often uses the word 'equanimous', and knew that our meditation experiences would yaw between feelings of rapture and dismay, even despair. Enjoy the pleasant sensations, but do not try to hang on to them – let them pass. Be aware of the painful sensations, but they will pass also. Develop a mind that treats all sensations equally, with no preference, and equanimity will be achieved.

I will never forget those ten days. Completely without any human interaction – without family, friends or work colleagues, with no newspapers and books, no emails or phone – just me with my prejudices, fears and biases to keep me company and which, it turned out, were useless. Wayward thoughts might still buzz around your head as you try to meditate, but coming back to the breath and body, again and again, you experience the sub-atomic particles Goenka mentioned, pulsing harmoniously through your being. It is an ineffable experience. It wasn't easy: I nearly left on the fifth day after the morning session, because I had spent that time with my mind in a kind of fugue, but in the evening session, when I least expected it, I had my epiphany. I experienced a deep, peaceful and harmonious meditation state, and I knew I had to stay. By surrendering totally, I was now devoid of all expectations.

In one of the last sessions of Vipassana, I had an unexpected cathartic experience which resulted in a reconciliation with my late mother. Growing up as one of nine siblings, she had not shown me the affection or love I thought I deserved and expected, and I believed that in her relationship with her five daughters, she exhibited a preference for them. Although I knew our father abnegated his basic fatherhood responsibilities and she did the best she could with little money, I couldn't help but be resentful and angry. As I grew older, sensing this, my siblings would gently remind me of her struggles in raising us all singlehandedly, and I gradually accepted the situation that had occurred. My mother had been gone many years by the time of my Vipassana experience, and there was only a residual memory left of my old resentment or anger. I was deep into a meditation when something happened which was extraordinary, almost psychedelic. With my eyes closed, I was joined via what I could only describe as an umbilical cord, which was in my mind, and was connected to my mother, now long dead. I felt a great release and peace, and I was not separate from her but part of her. How could I have experienced so much negativity about her when I was always a part of her? I understood now. I didn't experience guilt about my feelings towards my mother, I just felt relief and happiness at the resolution brought about by a session of meditation.

The vow of silence was rescinded on the eleventh day after the final early morning session. The noise as I walked into the dining room for breakfast was deafening, as 150 people, silent for ten days, released their voices, all wanting to convey to one another, as loudly as possible, their Vipassana experience; an uplifting, fitting end to the course. A coach load of people left the course that day, bound for Gloucester railway station, and from there we went our separate ways. I was, as many others were, I suppose, on a sort of 'high'. I wasn't ready for the real world. On the train, there was a young mother with a child of maybe three years old, and she appeared harassed, stressed. I wanted to tell her it needn't be like that, but what practical use would that be? She couldn't give up ten days of her life to go and meditate.

I remember a passage from Tim Park's book: when a fellow meditator at the end of the course asked the course leader what he should do now that it had ended, he appeared at a loss. I never felt that way. For some time afterwards, I suppose I was a 'Vipassana bore', evangelically mentioning to everyone I met the virtues of Vipassana meditation. Mostly, I was met with a polite response when I talked about Vipassana, and puzzlement from some that I should have undertaken it at all. I soon grew to realise that trying to explain the Vipassana experience was impossible – you could explain how you thought it had changed you, but that was not really the point. The experience had to be experienced – there was no other way.

On Lake O, I changed from the buzzer patterns to a Gold Ribbed Hairs Ear nymph – a fly using the fur from the inside of a hare's ear. Now it's used as a nymph pattern with a rib of gold wire or tinsel along its body, but it was originally concocted by Francis Francis and James Ogden in the mid-1800s as a dry fly, a winged Blue Dun. Today the thorax of the nymph is picked out by a dubbing needle to resemble the legs, or branchiae. It is still a must-have pattern in your fly box, crowded as it is.

I am sure my friend had long exhausted the adrenaline reserves in his body, because we had observed him playing a trout for over two hours, at times towing him along with his float tube. The trout eventually escaped, and we worked with our fins towards him. With a foul-hooked trout, which is when a hook has gained a purchase in the tail or body, the fight it gives can make you think you have hooked a leviathan. They become so powerful because they can use their streamlined body and the thrust of their tail. I rarely net one, as they straighten the hook and flee. But no, he hadn't foul-hooked the fish, yes, he had glimpsed it and it wasn't one of the lake monsters, yes, he was glad he had lost the fight.

To practice playing a fish you basically have to have a fish on, and then it's not practice, it's for real. A dog, it turns out, is a poor substitute for a fish. One winter, at the Blue Quill fly shop in Evergreen, Colorado, a few of us went out back and tried playing Dixie on an eight weight fly rod. Dixie was a lean, young, fun-loving forty-pound mutt who had done this before: a game with the humans where she is the centre of attention. Dixie's owner tied the leader to the dog's collar, handed the rod to my friend, A.K. Best and then threw an old slobbered-on tennis ball far out into the open field. A.K. said it felt just like the first run of a big striped bass. Naturally, I had to try it and when the dog took off I instinctively dipped the rod tip and even felt a little of that helplessness that grips you when the reel starts to scream and you think you've hooked something you might not be able to land. But then Dixie just picked up the ball and trotted back faster than I could reel in line, so it was sort of anticlimactic. Finally, someone wandered out and said, "You guys haven't been fishing for a while, have you?" I suddenly felt embarrassed and went inside for coffee.

My friend's two-hour contest was the longest I had ever witnessed. During that time I had caught three good rainbow trout. With a strengthening wind and some drizzle now, it was time to curtail any further fishing in the float tube, and we ended our Lake O experience.

The life-changing experience of Vipassana enabled me to gain acceptance of those days in my competitive career when, as a team member competing against other teams, I would come in at the end of a competition with fewer fish – sometimes no fish, though that was rare – than other members of my team. They had caught more, had done better than me and in the past I would have inwardly beaten my-self up in letting the team down. We were all friends, and no criticism was ever implied by any team members – it could happen to anyone of us. I relate these experiences now to Kipling's Poem 'If':

> If you can meet with Triumph and Disaster
> And treat those two impostors just the same

I had achieved this equanimous state of mind. After the Vipassana experience, results were important, but they no longer affected me very much on a personal level.

| 3 |

Cutthroats in Yellowstone

Pheasant Tail Nymph

When I was a boy, I always wanted explanations of how things were made, how things functioned. My parents were constantly exasperated by me taking apart all sorts of items, then being unable or unwilling to put them together again. For all that, I left school at fifteen with no qualifications and no idea about what I should do. But it was the Sixties, and back then anything seemed possible. I grew up as a prolific reader of Science Fiction, then moved onto Dostoyevsky, Steinbeck and Hemingway. I tried my hand at writing, inspired by Steinbeck's *The Grapes of Wrath*, but most of my experiences were read about in books, not lived.

It is easy to become inspired by Dickens or Steinbeck, and what is there in human experience that hasn't been mined in literature? Two of the most sublime and memorable quotes ever written open and close a classic by Dickens: "It was the best of times, it was the worst of times" and "It is a far, far better thing that I do, than I have ever done; it is a far, far better rest that I go to than I have ever known." This final line of *A Tale of Two Cities* is spoken by Sidney Carton, a flawed and complex character, as he prepares to make the ultimate sacrifice for a friend. Dickens' portrayal suspends disbelief and allows us to entirely accept something of which we might otherwise question the likelihood or reality. In the last moments of Steinbeck's masterpiece *The Grapes of Wrath* the Joad family, destitute, wet and hungry, find shelter in an old barn, where they find a father and son who are starving. The father has given any food they found to his son, and is now dying of hunger. A bereaved young mother in the Joad family puts her breasts to the dying man's lips, and feeds him. In this moment of pure humanity, the book ends. What could these examples of fiction do but inspire me also to write? But inspiration alone doesn't write books, and I think these marvellous works of fiction in fact shackled me. I knew that in my late teens, with my lack of personal life experience, writing good fiction would be beyond me.

Growing older, I read more non-fiction, and now read as much by the likes of Richard Dawkins and Christopher Hitchens as by Gore Vidal or Philip Roth. I wanted to understand the enigmas of consciousness, brain function and how personality is shaped by outside influences. I came across Professor Bruce Hood when I read his book *The Self Illusion*, which has allowed me to begin to understand how so many of the influences in childhood and beyond shape who we become, and make us who we are.

I was born in Germany, when the family was in married quarters at an RAF base, where Dad worked. I grew up as the middle child of nine, moving frequently to wherever our father was posted. The one constant was our religion, Catholicism. I recall that for a long time the happiest day of my life was the day of my first holy communion, when I believed that Christ had inhabited my body. I was seven years old. If I had been aware then of Bruce Hood's "there is no you inside your head", I might have come to the realisation that 'there is no Christ inside your body'. I was, as all children are, a product of my upbringing, and in my case a product of religious dogma forced onto me by well-meaning parents. So there it was, the self illusion was alive and kicking, and living in me. In his book, Bruce Hood points out:

> Our identity is the sum of our memories but it turns out that memories are fluid, modified by context and simply confabulated. This means we cannot trust them and our sense of self is compromised. Note how this leaves us with a glaring paradox – without a sense of self, memories have no meaning and yet the self is a product of our memories.

Growing up, it wasn't until I was fifteen that I declared I would no longer go to church, and freed myself from the Saturday confessions I made to the priest in the confessional. The guilty secrets spilt out to the priest by an adolescent, riven by doubts and insecurities, went far in undermining self-confidence and self-esteem at a time when both were critical to a boy trying to make sense of the world.

Professor Bruce Hood is a Canadian-born British experimental psychologist who specialises in developmental cognitive neuroscience in children. He has a PhD from Cambridge, worked as a professor at MIT and Harvard, and currently works at Bristol University teaching Developmental Psychology. He is no slouch. In 2012, he published *The Self Illusion: Why there is no 'You' inside your Head*. What is this 'self' that, according to him, we should regard as illusory? I think I know what my 'self' is – that I am able to exercise free will – I am an independent entity. Although I recognise that both influences of nature and nurture have helped mould me, this self is somehow still 'me', for all of the effect they have had. But Hood states otherwise: "we are not who we think we are", we are completely affected not by our personality, uniqueness, but what our brain has absorbed through learned experiences in childhood through to adulthood. His book resonates with ideas in Jiddu Krishna-murti's book *Freedom from the Known*, that true freedom and knowledge of self can only begin if we cast off all the learnt paraphernalia accumu-lated through the years – a tall order, maybe. Both are saying, in their different ways, that in theory a person, you or I, cannot ever know his or her true individual uniqueness: Hood, because no one can ever escape the shackles of the learnt experience, and Krishnamurti, because he recognises this truth but theorises that abandoning all known learnt experiences would allow an individual to discover the true 'self'.

> I am not what I think I am and I am not what you
> think I am, I am, what I think that you think I am.

In the third chapter of his book, Hood quotes this tongue-twister from the American sociologist Charles Horton Cooley as an example of how some people shape themselves to fit other people's perceptions. What about free will? Surely in exercising free will we confound Cooley's point, as we choose not to engage with the prejudicial and judgmental influences of others? Oh, if it could be so simple! When we exercise free will, we are choosing within the confines of the learnt experiences, our memories, our genetic disposition, our biases, what our current circumstances are, and how we think any decision might affect our future. Can any decision predicated on these factors be free? Professor Hood quotes the seventeenth century philosopher Baruch Spinoza: "Men are mistaken in thinking themselves free; their opinion is made up of consciousness of their own actions and ignorance of the causes by which they are determined."

On a scientific television programme some years ago, scientists were imaging a brain whilst a person answered questions producing a YES or NO response. They were able to pinpoint the areas of the brain that lit up when a YES or NO answer was given, but more interestingly, these areas lit up *before* that person consciously answered. The brain scan showed that the person's brain was aware of what the person would choose before they consciously chose it. If our consciousness is subordinate to unconscious factors, then how can free will operate freely? I wondered, could this be where hunches are born? Maybe a hunch is something between this subconscious-conscious state of awareness? Hunches happen to me sometimes when I arrive at a fishery with no clear idea of what fly to tie onto my cast, and amongst the myriad of choices in my fly box, I seem to know with a kind of certainty what fly will be successful. Then again, this hunch isn't always correct.

A couple of years before this study, Jane Elliot, a third-grade teacher in Iowa, America, performed her own study based on eye-colour. One day she told her class that there was very good evidence that children with blue eyes were superior to students with brown eyes. Following this revelation, Elliot afforded the blue-eyed students privileges, such as extra-long breaks and being first in the lunch queue. However, the next day, she said she had been wrong, and that in fact the evidence proved that brown-eyed children were superior. This role reversal produced the same pattern. On both days, children who were designated as inferior took on the look and behaviour of genuinely inferior students, performing poorly on tests, whereas the superior group became more hostile to the inferior group, thinking them less worthy. The study proved that simply belonging to a group influences how you feel about yourself, and about others not in your group.

The fascinating simplicity of the experiment related to eye colour was developed further by the work of Henri Tajfel, who used to be head of Hood's department and who devised a simple experiment with Bristol schoolchildren, which was to override this idea of 'self' in favour of group membership: he simply divided them into two groups by the toss of a coin. This produced changes in the way that they treated each other, even though all of them belonged to the same class. Within the group members became more positive towards each other, and hostile to the members of the other group.

Of course, these experiments shine a light on how susceptible human nature is to the concept of the 'other' as inherently bad or wrong, without any need for any actual wrongdoing from that group. Such unsubstantiated biases and prejudices are at the heart of twentieth century nationalism and countless conflicts and genocides, from Japan to Western Europe, Cambodia to Rwanda. These experiments demonstrate that tribal hatred can happen naturally, even when it is entirely arbitrary, so it is not surprising so see it so often used as a tool to justify or excuse marginalisation of social, racial and religious groups across the world. Added to this, when there is something to be gained from silencing or discriminating against another group, this naturally occurring belief that the 'other' must in some way be wrong, allows injustices to be upheld even in cases where there is a clear and seemingly objective wrong in place.

When four of us decided to fly fish in Montana rivers, the Little Blackfoot and the Beaverhead came up in our search parameters. We decided to go to Yellowstone National Park, which is partly in Montana. Yellowstone also straddles Wyoming and Idaho, and is unique geologically and geographically. Native Americans inhabited the area for thousands of years, until gold was found in the Black Hills and the United States government reneged on the 1868 Fort Laramie Treaty that had ceded the lands to the Sioux. It was a deliberate abrogation that has been the centre of legal debate ever since, and in which the United States shows a profound lack of honour and truthfulness. "We'd like to see that land back" says Chief John Spotted Tail, speaking at the unveiling a display of the Fort Laramie Treaty of 1868, at the National Museum of the American Indian. In five generations since the treaty was signed and broken, the Sioux Nations steadily lost reservation lands to white development. They now live in small reservations scattered throughout the region. "From the time we signed, we were put into poverty and to this day our people are still in poverty," Spotted Tail says. "We're a third world country out there. The United States does not honour this treaty and continues to break it, but as Lakota people, we honour it every day." Disenfranchised and ill-treated by the U.S. government on numerous occasions due to the breaking of treaties signed by the United States government and Native Americans, surely history wouldn't repeat itself? Well, it seems it always does. In 2017 the treaties of 1851 and 1868 were violated when Donald Trump agreed that the Keystone KXL pipeline could go ahead across lands ceded to the Rosebud Sioux Tribe.

I wanted to fish the streams and rivers of the American mid-west. My appetite was whetted by the books of John Gierach, who Americans affectionately call 'the patron saint of fly fishers'. A writer of twenty books chronicling a fly fishing life by the waters of Colorado, Montana, Idaho and Wyoming, his books are written in a pared-down prose that is witty, descriptive, sometimes lyrical, but self-effacing. I loved them. He didn't offer up too many of the names of the rivers (who can blame him for that), but in one of his elegiac pieces he mentioned 'Henry's Fork', a tributary of the Snake River. I had heard from other sources that it was like the River Test, but two or three times the size of our cherished water. I wrote to him for some advice about where to access this 127-mile river, and he replied with useful suggestions. This time, though, we would forgo a visit to Henry's Fork.

in 1872, Yellowstone became the first National Park in the United States. Comprised of lakes, valleys, canyons, rivers, forests and mountain ranges, the area is nearly half the size of Wales, contains 290 waterfalls, and is the largest volcanic system in North America. The magma chamber that lies under Yellowstone measures 60 kilometres by 29 kilometres, and is at some points 12 kilometres deep. The Yellowstone Caldera is home to a supervolcano, and when (rather than if, according to some geologists) an eruption happens, the ash deposited in the atmosphere will alter the climate around the globe. Half of the world's geysers and hydrothermal features are concentrated in Yellowstone, the most famous being 'Old Faithful'. The Continental Divide mountain ridge runs through the park. Although the origins of the Snake and Yellowstone Rivers are close, they are opposite sides of the 'Divide', so the waters of the Snake River flow into the Pacific, while the Yellowstone flows into the Atlantic Ocean, via the Gulf of Mexico. Sixty-seven species of mammals, three hundred species of birds and many different species of amphibians, reptiles and fish live in Yellowstone. The Lamar Valley situated there is often referred to as 'America's Serengeti', and its inhabitants include two wolf packs as well as pronghorn, bison and bear. Half of the four million people visiting annually come in the summer months. Wheeled vehicles are banned in winter, with snowmobiles and snowcoaches being the only way of travel.

We were there in a year of more forest fires than usual. Roads were closed and the distant smoke we encountered in the day morphed into flames at night. There were also concerns about bears: two days previously, I had watched a tourist couple chasing a bear and her cub up a steep incline, trying to get a photo of them. We were in one of several cars that stopped, witnessing with a mixture of horror and disbelief as they tried to gain traction on the wet slippery incline of the bluff to catch up with the animal. Luckily for them, it was hopeless, and the bear soon lost her pursuers. Bears will indeed avoid humans at all costs, but it is best not to surprise one walking through the woods, so we made as much noise as we could to announce ourselves. We had no pepper spray – the deterrent of choice – but it turned out that none was necessary.

We had come to fish the Lamar River, just 40 miles long, and only fishable in late summer, after the long period of high water had subsided, when the river started to show its bones. Now we could see the gravel beds and shingle that was no longer covered by water. Close by, larger rocks the size of small boulders were stacked up in piles the height of one of the banks, forced there by water from the winter snowmelt, the source that created and fed the river. The river itself is famous for cutthroat trout, named for a distinctive red 'slash' below its jaws. We were there to try to catch this fish that I had only glimpsed in photos in the fishing magazines. I had waded into the cold, clear water about ten feet from the bank, and was casting upstream with a single nymph pattern called a Pheasant Tail nymph, appropriately tied with Cock Pheasant tail fibres. It represented an emerging Baetis, or Olive nymph. This fly has a worldwide reputation for catching fish that may never have seen an Olive nymph. It is 'the' universal fly pattern, able to tempt fish regardless of what other food is in the water, and was invented by Frank Sawyer some 60 years ago.

Frank Sawyer was born in Bulford, Wiltshire in 1906. When he was nineteen, Sawyer was employed as Assistant Riverkeeper on the Hampshire Avon, then, as now, a world-class Chalkstream. Three years later, he became Head Riverkeeper of the Services Dry Fly Fishing Association, a fly fishing club for the Armed Forces, and remained in the post for another fifty years. Sawyer was a prolific writer, author of the classic book *Keeper of the Stream*, as well as hundreds of articles. His other fly 'inventions' included the Killer Bug, the Grey Goose nymph and the Bow Tie buzzer. The Killer Bug, or Grayling Bug as it was originally called, was tied with a wool called Chadwicks 477. When the production of this wool ceased in 1965, anglers worldwide began the search for a substitute. It was all about the shade of the wool. At times the colour could be matched, but when it became wet, the colour changed and looked different. A friendship developed between Sawyer and Oliver Kite, a master fisherman, writer and broadcaster of TV nature programmes, who then popularised the flies created by Sawyer.

However, the friendship soured. The reason why is lost in time. Some felt that that the men's competitive nature was such that each thought the other was riding on the coattails of their own fame. Whatever the reason, this rift drove them apart, and although they both lived nearby in Bulford, they hardly spoke to one another again. Kite died aged forty-eight of a second heart attack while on the River Test. Not much is known of Sawyer's private life, but he was married, and his wife, Marguerite, tied the patterns he created, which were sold commercially. In 1979, he was awarded an MBE for his contribution to fishing and conservation, and died a year later on the banks of his beloved River Avon.

I worked the Pheasant Tail nymph, quartering the water upstream, mending the flyline (moving it during the drift) to compensate for the 'bow' created by the river's flow. There were no rises to hatching flies, and little in the way of fly hatches. I wasn't surprised: there was a nip of autumn in the air even in late August. I persevered with the sunk nymph, a Copper Wire Rib weighing down the nymph pattern, but not enough to send it down to the bottom of the river. I had a take after about half an hour, then hooked one and landed my first Cutthroat trout after about an hour. When you catch a species for the first time it's a very special day, and looking at this trout with a body of yellow-brown and olive hues and a great red 'slash' along its jaw, I was elated. I quickly removed the barbless hook and returned it to the river. Cutthroat trout, native only to North America, although not on the endangered species list, are regarded as a sensitive species. Non-native species such as brook, brown and rainbow trout should be culled, the Yellowstone authorities insist, as they have led to the decline of the Cutthroat by accessing their larder and interbreeding with them. Despite this decline, Yellowstone has the largest population of Cutthroats in the world.

After fishing the Lamar, we fished the Madison River. Bigger than the Lamar, it is 140 miles long and its character changes throughout, from slow and meandering to white rapids. It runs into Quake Lake, which was formed in 1959 when an earthquake created a massive landslide. The landslide, which left 28 people dead, stopped the river, and the water backed up to create an ominous lake with spectral remains of trees, only their trunks remaining to push up through the water, enhancing its ghostly aspect. The Army engineers were able to cut a spillway so that the Madison could be released. Passing through Quake Lake and beneath the white-water rapids, the river is swift-flowing, and snow-capped mountains frame the skyline. It is beautiful.

We tried the Lamar using dry Daddy patterns (imitations of Daddy Long Legs), and then our old standby, Pheasant Tail nymphs, but remained fishless. As we were packing up, an osprey swooped by, passing horizontally along the river. Ospreys are rare in England, as rare as they are in America. They are slightly less rare in Scotland and Wales, and where they are found, the nests are protected with surveillance cameras and dedicated bird watchers. Before the Madison, I had only had glimpses of them through binoculars from 'Official Viewing Sites'. Its feet dipped into the water and out again, with a trout securely held in its huge claws. Now, there's a fisherman, I thought admiringly. I had watched kingfishers back home, so small and adept at catching on the small streams I use to fish, and these fish-catching birds are just magical to me.

I once said to a friend, "don't you wish you were John Gierach, fishing three or four times a week and then just writing about it?" He rebuked me — "no, I wouldn't want to be anyone but myself" — and of course, he was right. It is a foolish idea. I have sometimes tried to match what my competition partner is doing when we have fished in a boat together and he is catching and I am not. I know the fly-line he is using, have a fair idea of the flies on his cast and have watched his method of retrieve, and I copy all these assiduously, but with little or no success. Something small but different in what I am doing in copying him is cruelly rendering me fishless and I am at a loss to know what it could be. I learnt a lesson: do not presume to try on the clothes of another person by imitating his methods, but ignore him (and the success he is having – hard as that is) and fish in a way that comes naturally to you. It might not yield any fish, might be the day you come in fishless, but you have remained true to yourself, your own thought processes have prevailed, and you have not been hijacked by the influence of another person.

| 4 |

Grey Wulff on Lough Corrib

Grey Wulff

We had come, the four of us, to the West of Ireland to fish Lough Corrib, where we had rented a waterside lodge. I think we realised that we were privileged to be able to leave jobs and families for a fishing excursion to Ireland and other countries, but none of us were rich. We were, however, comfortable, and our careers were diverse but well paid: a retired fireman, a quantity surveyor, a physicist, and a company director (myself). Our party on the Corrib were members of the

Kingfishers, a club joined only by invitation, which had no membership fees and was the home of competent anglers. A few had written books on fly fishing, while others were internationals who fished for their country. We had two or three successful teams entering national and international fly fishing competitions, and social functions helped to knit all of us together. Few members of the Kingfishers were able to devote both time and money to these excursions abroad, and most had no inclination to do so, as the fishing they participated in met their needs for the most part. It was therefore a sort of natural selection that brought us together for these trips.

WC2, for that was his nickname, was Welsh and a retired fireman. Everyone called him WC2 as others would tell us quite regularly that he had been a Welsh fly fishing champion not once, but twice. He was married and had one son. Not tall, and quite rotund, his face was a touch on the florid side, but with sharp eyes peering out that never missed much, especially where fishing was concerned. He was exceptional at spotting fish that were rising. He was the joker of our small party, and the most catholic of us when it came to fishing: he would use any lure or attractor flies to catch fish, while the rest of us, who were more purist, used only nymphs or dry flies.

Matthew, who had just entered his sixth decade, worked as a quantity surveyor, and was married with no children. He was a big man and seemed to be on a never-ending diet. With red hair and a face full of freckles, he shunned the sun as much as possible, as he was prone to sunburn very easily. Matt was one of the finest fishermen I ever knew. Forensic in his attention to detail, probably a necessary quality needed in his job as a surveyor, the flies that he tied were to such a high standard that you could be forgiven in thinking they were real insects, they were so lifelike. He had acquired several English fly fishing caps, and one year was selected as a member of the English world fly fishing team, a select group comprised of just four people. Matthew, as the years went by, fished almost exclusively with dry flies, even if there was no activity on the water to suggest the fish were up and feeding. Fish would oblige him, doing things they wouldn't normally do, coming up from nowhere to take them.

John was of slim build and medium height. He had dark hair atop a face of sharply delineated features; a nose small and pointed, blue eyes, a square jaw. I guess he was the one person amongst us who could be described as handsome. He was a nuclear physicist working out of a power station near his home. The prodigious brainpower he possessed, he had adapted to his love of fly fishing, and he was quite brilliant at it. Earning several England caps, inventing new fly patterns and writing articles for the angling press made him, I think, the complete fisherman. Fishing mainly with dries, he would use other flies such as attractors, but he was a floating line specialist and hardly ever went down in the water with a sinking line for his fish. He never needed to, such was his skill. He possessed a dry wit that left you asking yourself whether a comment he made was, in fact, tongue-in-cheek.

We fished for the tug on the line, but had taken different journeys or evolutions to reach the point where we fished in similar ways, with imitative nymphs and dry flies. When I started fly fishing, I used wet flies – attractors and mini-lures that flashed through the water in a fast retrieve – and that was OK, but never as successful as when fish were presented with imitative flies that looked like food. I often see younger fisherman casting 25-30 yards, then stripping line back as fast as they can. If you can or want to do this for, say, ten minutes, then that is OK, but after hours or, as in competitions particularly, the whole day is spent on this technique, it will sap your upper body strength, which weakens the older you become. Usually, a mini-lure is used: one popular fly, a complete antithesis of an imitative one, is used a great deal: it is created by using the flashiest fly-tying material there is, wrapped around the hook. It is so bulbous that it almost obscures the barb of the hook and is aptly named 'The Blob'. This is for young men who also want to feel they have earned the fish they have caught. I am not physically able to adopt this method, but it can be very productive for stocked rainbow trout. Up against the resident brown trout here, on the Corrib, a waste of time: Corrib trout are switched onto one thing in their daily lives – food sources yielded up by the aquatic insects in the water. Uninterested in anything else, they would find a lure such as a 'blob' so un-foodlike they would ignore it. Whilst their stocky cousins in angling fisheries in the UK, not knowing what a 'blob' could be, and hoping it might be food, would be more eager to take it. Wild fish have too much self-esteem!

When I read Will Storr's book, *Selfie*, some years later, I realised that the Kingfishers Club I had joined was my 'tribe'. An early chapter called "The Tribal Self" describes how we are programmed by our upbringing to be individuals within a group or tribe. Reputation and standing can only be achieved in a tribe by caring what others think about you. It is this basic human preoccupation that prompts an individual's desire for inclusivity within a group. In my last chapter, the experiments by Hood and Tajfel highlighted how natural we find even arbitrary reasons to belong to a tribe, and also the outcomes of not being seen as part of any tribe, instead being seen as an 'other' or outsider.

So, what is a 'tribe'? I suppose it could be anything from being a supporter of your local team to a member of a narco gang, from being connected to a xenophobic organisation to being native to the Amazon rainforest. Or just a member of a fishing club. Tribal pressures explain, I think, why a person will vote for the same political party through-out their life, no matter what, and 'class', although its effects have diminished in recent history, still exerts a strong tribal force for many people. Families are hugely tribal, and in-laws sometimes don't make the cut, something I experienced when I joined my wife in Spain for a week to celebrate a big number birthday for her sister. There was a very strong contingent of her family and extended family present, and the interactions were quite naturally strongest amongst their group. I wasn't excluded, but neither was I wholly included. I'm certain my spouse has the same experience at social occasions with my family. In recent years, social media has helped to form and bind tribes together. My wife's family are ardent users of this format, whereas my family are not. Recent birthday greetings on Facebook for a member of her family numbered over sixty, mine somewhat less!

Paradoxically, social media promotes and celebrates the individual ego, redoubling the focus of each member of the social group on how they are perceived and how they would like to be perceived. Will Storr is an award-winning investigative journalist and novelist, and I am a fan of his. His book *Selfie: How We Became So Self-Obsessed and What It's Doing to Us* is a multi-layered critique of our Western values, the origins of which can be traced back to the individualism of ancient Greece. Over the next two and a half thousand years, he takes us through misguided Christian ideals, Freudian influences, to how we have arrived at our present state. Reviewing *Selfie*, Antony Gottlieb, a Fellow of All Souls College, Oxford, wrote that "worrying about one's own narcissism has a whiff of paradox. If we are suffering from self-obsession, should we really feed the disease by poring over another book about ourselves? Well, perhaps just one more." He is right; there are too many truths in this book to ignore.

Storr concludes that the focus on the all-consuming need of the individual which spawned the 'Me Generation', its excessive and un-earned self-esteem, and the quest for perfectionism, has its roots in the 1960s at the Esalen Institute in Big Sur California, in what became known as the 'Human Potential Movement'. The movement posited that personal and societal 'ills' would be cured by freeing ourselves from the straitjacket of religion and other dogma, in favour of personal human growth and the latent spirituality exposed by their 'self-love' programmes. Will Storr would agree that this in itself wasn't world changing, but he discovered a link that was. In 1986, after attending programmes at the Esalen Institute, John Vasconcellos, a Californian State Congressman, persuaded Governor George Deukmejian to fund a task force to promote self-esteem as a means of naturally promoting personal and social responsibility. Professors at the University of California would create self-esteem programmes to counter homelessness, drug abuse and crime, and people would realise their true self-value and potential. The scheme was met with widespread derision at the time, but in 1989, the Emeritus Professor of Sociology at Berkeley, Dr Neil Smelser, responsible for coordinating the work of the seven professors, published what seemed to be impeccable academic research that low self-esteem was linked to social problems. This was just what the task force had hoped for: a year later they published their own report and their publicists went into overdrive to promote it, with further endorsements from Oprah Winfrey and even Bill Clinton. Unfortunately, although some correlations were indicated, there was no solid evidence of causation. For example, drug abuse might cause low self-esteem, rather than low self-esteem leading to drug use. No-one wanted to point out that the "impeccable academic research" was being misrepresented by the Esalen Institute's publicists. As Antony Gottlieb commented, "perhaps those involved in the deception had too much self-esteem to be ashamed of what they had done".

Western attitudes are slowly pervading Eastern cultural mores, which were typically less individualistic and more societally directed. For example, in the Second World War, Japanese Soldiers were dismissive of British POWs because they did not kill themselves, but rather allowed themselves to be taken prisoner. Western individualistic standards meant they were more important as individuals than the society they represented, whereas the Japanese, if captured, felt they had let down their society, and therefore saw their death as the only reasonable outcome. Societal, cultural pressures are all-consuming. No-one can escape them, in a way because we cannot see them, as fish cannot see the ocean.

A famous study conducted by Stanley Milgram demonstrated that a group of ordinary people, asked to give increasingly strong electric shocks to another group when they got a question wrong, would follow the instructions even to the point that the shocks were at a lethal level. It was all a set-up, of course: no electric shocks were given, and actors were employed to pretend they were receiving them. However, the participants were willing to follow potentially dangerous orders because people in white coats, respected in our culture, were telling them to do so. 'Following orders' is of course famously used in attempts to excuse soldiers, workers and even civilians at the height of the Nazi concentration camps. However, this pattern doesn't only occur when there are grave consequences for disobeying. The people in Milgram's study would have risked nothing by refusing to continue. Even with less at stake, we have all blindly trusted or followed instructions in the face of our own common sense. If we need further proof, we need only look at people who drive into fields, lakes and even more dangerous places because their sat-nav told them to.

Social pressures vary not only between cultures but even within them. For example, the age of perfectionism in Western culture puts different pressures on different genders: men should be provider, protector, winner, fighter, someone who never loses control, who doesn't show vulnerability; women are wife, mother or earner who should be extroverted, individualistic, slim, hard-working and socially aware, an entrepreneur. If ideals of selfhood in both sexes are not being achieved – and how could they be – then there is a discrepancy between who we are and who we feel we ought to be, paradoxically creating low self-esteem by striving for high self-esteem as an expectation, the driver of social perfectionism. According to Will Storr, "the lie at the heart of the age of perfectionism is that we can be anything we want to be". His message: stop trying to change ourselves, as we are only what our genes, environment and tribe have made us, and focus instead on worthwhile ways to change the world.

Lough Corrib is the largest lake in the Republic of Ireland. It is huge, and its 176 square kilometres are thought to contain 365 islands (in fact a recent GPS survey found a total of 1327, though I would think many of those are no more than rock outcrops). It is one of the world's great game fisheries, and in its long season from February to the end of September, it can be fished for wild brown trout and salmon using a variety of methods. March sees the first fly hatches of chironomids, called duckfly by the locals, but we knew them as buzzers. In spring, salmon and grilse runs appear, and are usually caught by trolling a bait behind a moving boat. April sees the first hatches of olives – a smaller member of the mayfly family. Mayflies start hatching in late May through to June, leading to a new, non-artificial method of fishing, as the boatmen pay schoolchildren to collect the plentiful mayfly from the surrounding vegetation. Alive, the unfortunate mayfly are skewered onto hooks, presented on floss dapping lines and long rods, and the lightweight lines are blown rather than cast, along with their passengers, onto the water. The trout eat these up with gusto and are hooked.

We were not there for that; live baiting was something I was not prepared to do. Our world abounds with ill-treatment of our fellow creatures, and I will not insert a treble hook into the flanks of a mackerel so that a bigger fish is tempted by the mackerel's distress and takes it as bait. However, controversy still abounds about the ability of fish to feel pain. A report published in *Science Daily* in 2013 by an international team of neurobiologists, behavioural ecologists and fishery scientists, concluded that fish do not feel pain the same way that humans do, as they lack the neuro-physiological capacity to be conscious of pain. Another, contradictory report, issued by the Smithsonian Institute, claims that fish suffer a 'form' of physical pain. I don't think that I would have remained a fisherman if I believed that fish were susceptible to physical pain, for I have caught a trout that has probably previously been attacked by a pike, with their insides hanging out of their stomach, still willing to take a nymph I presented to them. Compared to a soldier in battle with a similar condition, I am sure no thoughts of feeding would intrude.

Similarly, inserting a hook in the lip of a human and pulling would create no resistance – the person would go wherever the pressure wanted him to. A fish, when hooked, will start to pull and resist against the pressure until too tired to continue. I am sure they do feel fear and I ensure that I do not delay their capture by 'playing' them for too long. I have always felt uneasy subjecting living beings to unnecessary cruelty. I know that trawlers emptying the seas of fish have no other way to kill their catch, other than allowing them to thrash around the decks until they die of suffocation, and I accept that, as I do abattoirs – I must accept it if I want to include meat and fish in my diet. Yet I think it is a hideous and cruel practice to cut away fins from a shark and then throw the shark overboard to die because of a demand for shark fin soup. I hope that most fishermen feel the same way. I will take a fish for the table when trout fishing. The fish is dispatched by a short, heavy club-like implement called a priest, which administers the last rites by a blow to the back of its head. I play it quickly to avoid unnecessary distress and as soon as it is landed, even before I take it out of the net, it is dispatched with the priest.

The Southern Corrib is shallower than its Northern counterpart, and has, in places, rocks just below the waterline and a long way from the shoreline where you might expect them – disconcerting when you see them almost scraping the bottom of your boat. For this reason, a local boatman and his knowledge of the lake's topography is vital. Tragedies often occur on water. In September 1828 a boat left Annagh-down Pier with thirty men and women, bound for a fair in Galway. It was a highlight in the social calendar for the souls on board. The story is that one of the sheep on board became restless and poked his hoof through the floor of the boat. In trying to stuff the hole with his over-coat, one of the men succeeded only in knocking a plank completely out and causing water to pour in. Nineteen people lost their lives, the sheep also.

Michael, an old friend, was our boatman today. All the Corrib boat-men I had met could be described as 'characters' and I and he was no exception. He was in his mid-sixties, with a dry and taciturn sense of humour, and the Corrib had been his mistress for many years. He would describe the rough swells (a feature of this huge water) as a corduroy ripple, a torrential downpour as soft rain, and eschewed min-imum comforts such as a foam cushion, instead sitting for ten hours or so on a hard wooden transom or a thwartboard. Now Michael only ghillied with friends, or at least people he had known for many years and didn't actively dislike. He was hard to engage in conversation if the subject wasn't fishing-related, and rarely expressed opinions until later, in the pub, when Guinness would loosen a flow of very funny Irish jokes. A private, self-deprecating man, he engendered friendships and endeared himself to those that grew to know him.

It was mid-April and he was taking us to Ballynalty Bay, which appeared an inconsequential 'nick' on the map of Corrib but was bigger than most reservoirs in the UK. We were going to catch trout feeding on the hatching olives. He steered us through the treacherous rocks that litter the mouth of the bay and, on a fine late morning – it was to blow a hooley the next day – set us up on a drift. There is nothing like the anticipation of a good fishing day to come, and we hurried to tackle up. I had, however, become aware that there were no hatching flies and no trout moving on the surface. Trout rarely oblige the whims of fisherman. I started with a green nymph of my own tying, and fished subsurface. We had been fishing for about 30 minutes when I heard Michael shout "strike!" and saw my disconsolate fishing partner looking at a swirl in the water, where a fish had rejected his dry fly. These trout were not surface feeding, but they would come to a fly fished dry. I changed to a Grey Wulff, the fly I knew my buddy was using on the point, transferring the green nymph to a dropper. Michael's enthusiasm hadn't dimmed with age and his shouts of "fish here" or "fish there" as he spotted trout rising reminded us to keep our wits about us. Michael expected certain standards from his fishermen.

Henry Leon Wulff was born in Alaska in 1905. He was the inventor of many flies, including the Grey Wulff. His father, participating in the Gold Rush at that time, didn't strike it rich – he became a deputy sheriff and a newspaperman in the small frontier town of Valdez. Lee, as the sheriff's son became known, started fishing at an early age. When he was twenty one he studied art at an academy in Paris, before returning to Greenwich Village. He moved to various states during the years that followed, and in his long career he was an artist, inventor, explorer, author, pilot, filmmaker and conservationist. But he will probably be best known as America's premier and most famous fisherman. He was also an extraordinary fly-tyer. Consider this: fly tying – you clamp a vice to a table and insert a bare hook into the 'nose' of the vice, which holds it securely. You proceed to tie various furs and feathers around the hook shank to produce the finished fly using both hands. A vice is essential — except in Lee Wulff's case, he didn't bother – holding the hook in one hand, he skillfully created a fly with the other one. I have been fly tying for many years and would be aghast if someone suggested I even give it a go!

Wulff was one of the original conservationists. He had the foresight to see that man's actions towards the environment were slowly eliminating the fish that he loved catching. He is famously quoted as saying:

> The finest gift you can give to any fisherman is to put a good fish back and who knows if the fish that you caught isn't someone else's gift to you. Game fish are too valuable to be caught only once.

He married world fly casting champion and avid fly angler Joan Salvato in 1967, and twelve years later they set up the Wulff school of fly fishing on the Beaverkill River in the Catskill mountains. He died in 1991 when the Piper Super Cub plane he was piloting crashed into trees at the end of the runway. Max Francisco, a flight instructor on board to check that Wulff, then in his eighty-sixth year, was still able to fly, survived the crash. He believed Wulff had suffered a stroke or heart attack, and was probably dead before the plane crashed into the trees. His death was the cause of the accident and not the result. Obituaries appeared in the *New York Times* and the *Guardian* newspaper; Charles Kuralt, host of CBS Television's show *Sunday Morning*, stated "Lee Wulff was to fly fishing what Einstein was to Physics".

The fishing that morning was excellent. I had caught two on the Grey Wulff and missed another couple, but my partner, an outstanding fisherman, had landed five and also missed a few. Seven to the boat is an exceptional day on Corrib. We were catching wild brown trout that required a higher skillset than the rainbow stockies back home. We returned them all unharmed, left Ballynalty Bay after lunch on the boat and went to Greenfields, through the tunnel under the road bridge to Inchiquin Island. White clouds, fluffy like mashed potatoes, appeared on the horizon, and a stiff breeze sprung up that started to chill us, although Michael seemed oblivious to it. The fishing had gone 'off' in the last few hours. The warmth of the Lodge and curiosity as to how our friends had fared tipped the balance, and we headed for home.

Few, if any, countries match the Irish in friendliness and hospitality. Although not the reason for our trip, this helped to make our Irish adventure so memorable. I never tire of the company, but am exhausted by the end. Irish pubs are like no others. I frequented some when I lived in Spain but they were not real Irish pubs, where the fiddler plays on regardless of the wall of noise, everyone seems to be talking at the same time, and there is an incredible buzz, an atmosphere I have never experienced elsewhere. We drank too much Guinness on our last night. Fortunately, Michael, friend and boatman, had arranged for someone to drive us all to Knock Airport, given that we were all of a fragile disposition, and that was good of him.

| 5 |

Salmon fishing in Scotland

Allys Shrimp

One of the most influential men who helped me immensely in my early days as a fly fisherman was Colin, who came to use my company's circular saw. He was well into his sixties – I was just twenty-six – and worked as a handyman in a company just across the road from our premises. Colin encouraged me a great deal, and persuaded me to join a local fishing club, of which he was life president. There, I learnt to tie flies and began to fish with more experienced fishermen. It was good to be amongst like-minded people. Although I missed the blessed solitude of fishing on my own, I had learnt more in a month as a club member than in the previous year. We had a once-weekly meeting in a room above a pub which hosted fly-tying demonstrations and talks by prominent fishermen.

The club was populated by some great personalities and the weekly social gatherings were often raucous. Most of these members erred on the extroverted side and although the club I joined later, the King-fishers, had better fishermen amongst its members, it was all about the fishing and not so much fun. My business partner and his twin brother were members, and though not identical twins, it was hard to tell them apart, which was fodder for comical misinterpretations. One of our members, Lewis, a painter and decorator, was the most honest man I have yet met, which could sometimes be disconcerting. He was apt to say exactly what he thought, whilst others, myself included, might keep such thoughts in our heads. He became a sort of bellwether figure, and a popular one at that. You couldn't get upset with Lewis, even if you didn't agree with him, because you had to recognise within him a rare, expressive honesty.

Competitions were arranged at various local fisheries, with three to a boat and three on the bank. Names drawn out of a hat decided your boat partner. Competition was good-humoured and not taken too seriously, although one angler, who had a history of wrapping his cast and flies around his unfortunate partners' heads, took exception to his boat partner wearing a crash helmet. Onboard, the helmet came off, of course – he had made his point. Fly-tying competitions took place over the winter months, and were judged by a member who remains the best fly-tyer I have met – a man who, and it might be difficult to believe, suffered from Parkinson's disease. You watched him at the fly-tyer's vice as he brought his hand, shaking with quite severe tremors, closer to the hook and then, somehow, with us all transfixed by the sight of his jerking hand, produced the most exquisite, delicate-looking fly, far beyond our capabilities.

The club raised many thousands for the local children's hospital, but regrettably, it folded due to internal squabbles. Members left and the club declined. It is sad, but even in the most apparently like-minded of organisations, whether a fishing club or a political party, different points of view can harden into strong and implacable oppositions, even in the non-political and placid environment of a fishing club. I can't recall exactly what caused this final rupture or how it came about, but it effectively ended our club's existence. The initial decline, caused by a power struggle between several members which, in the end, no-one won, is a salutary tale in this modern age of winner-takes-all. I still meet some of them at the bankside when fishing and it is always good to renew acquaintances.

Colin also taught me that all fishermen evolve and that expectations change. First comes the simple desire to catch a fish, then to catch as many fish as you can, then comes 'big fish syndrome': the desire for a bigger fish leads you to holes in the ground that are stocked with big but ugly fish with stunted tails and damaged scales, and you'll pay a lot of money to catch them, as fisheries recognise that they can cater to a fisherman's vanity. When I lived in Spain, I fished a river in the mountains stocked with huge broodfish. Along the walls of the café that issued the fishing permits were photos of grinning Spanish anglers holding grotesque caricatures of the ugliest fish I had ever seen. Beauty must be in the eye of the (be)holder! By then I had passed through that stage, into the sunny uplands of just wanting to catch specimen fish. The quantity and size didn't matter, only that the fish was well proportioned, had a full wide paddle of a tail and well defined, stream-lined flanks. Really, you could only catch these by catching wild fish, although some rainbow stockies in the larger reservoirs can mimic their wild cousins. Maybe I am being a touch judgmental, and I should remember a quote from Lee Wulff, "there will be no end to angling controversies for there is no best way for everyone to fish."

With that being said, none of the above makes any sense where salmon are concerned. The salmon angler is never going to catch a huge number, and it is serendipity that dictates the size of fish you catch, or whether it's a 'specimen' fish. The salmon angler, and I was one for a short while, just wants to catch a salmon, that is the sole criteria. To catch any species for the first time is special to a fisherman – to catch your first salmon is up there as one of the most memorable experiences of your life. You treat everyone to a whisky and have several yourself. A friend of mine, a good angler, spent a week a year for five years seeking salmon and never managed to hook one.

Atlantic salmon, one of seven species of salmon, are found in the Northern Atlantic and the rivers and streams of Western Europe from Northern Portugal to Norway, Iceland, Greenland, Russia, Great Britain, Canada and Alaska. All other species of salmon are native to the Pacific and are not found in Europe. Atlantic salmon breed in the adjacent rivers, and once their journey is complete, they die. The carcasses of millions of salmon nourish wildlife, such as bears, and enrich soils throughout Canada and Alaska. Some Atlantic salmon manage to survive the breeding excesses and will return to the sea, only to breed again in the river that they were born in. No one really knows how they are guided to the river of their birth, although some think that they locate this by the chemical signature of the river or stream. Another mystery about which no one is certain, is why, when Atlantic salmon will never feed in freshwater, do they take the fly we present to them? Maybe it's aggression, a territorial impulse, or just a distant memory of a shrimp worth grabbing at.

It is an early autumnal October day and I am fishing the River Beauly in Inverness-shire. It is mid-morning and this is my third day that week salmon fishing. This section of the Beauly runs through open countryside, edged by a few trees. To lower my profile, I wade out with the fast-flowing water. It exerts quite a force, and I am reluctant to go any deeper than waist-high, although I am wearing chest waders. I am no expert at salmon fishing or fishing big rivers, but there is one rule: before you start to wade, plan your exit. It is nearly impossible to turn around and exit the way you came because you are fighting against the flow of the water. You must go with the flow and angle your way back to the bank by going forward. You must be sure that there are no deep channels between you and the bank, otherwise you're in for a dunking, either by finding the deep water or turning back and losing the fight against the current. My ten-foot trout rod has been swapped for an old fourteen-foot salmon rod bought at a fishing club auction, and I cast the flyline downstream towards the middle of the river. The fly, pushed by the water's flow, swims across the river to end up near the bank. I move one step forward and recast. On my leader is a single hook fly called Ally's Shrimp.

Alastair Gowans, creator of Ally's Shrimp, is a fly fishing instructor, guide, lecturer, photographer, travel writer and author, who also has an engineering degree from Dundee University. He lives near Pitlochry in the Scottish Highlands and has been fishing for over fifty years and in many countries. He conducts tuition courses on trout fishing and has produced a number of articles and DVDs around fishing methods. An expert fly-tyer, he demonstrates his skills and fishing club meetings around the country. Whilst on a trawler he noticed that prawns were slim, long and moved quite quickly. In deciding to copy this, he produced his now world-famous salmon fly, Ally's Shrimp. It was not the first shrimp pattern for salmon – the General Practitioner, created in 1955 by Lt Colonel Esmund Drury, is still in use today – but Ally's Shrimp, with a slimmer profile and longer tail, is fished throughout the world's salmon rivers, has a listing in the *World's Best Flies* published by the North Atlantic Salmon Fund, and was voted the salmon fly of the millennium by the readers of the magazine, *Trout and Salmon*. A no-brainer, why would you not fish this fly?

I had a fly that (I hoped) would help to compensate for my lack of salmon fishing experience. When I felt a slight tightening on the line, heart in mouth, I waited. I waited because experienced salmon fishermen advocate that you hold a loop of the flyline and drop it when a fish is felt, to give the fish enough slack on which to turn before the hook is pulled home. The slack is taken up, and raising the rod sets the hook. The wait of a few seconds seems like an eternity. This is probably the one chance you will get to hook a salmon – the trout fisherman's mindset of 'Ah well, missed that one, there'll be another one along later' has no place here! Fish for a week and sometimes you don't get a sniff to your fly. Anyhow, I had hooked a salmon, and now I had to land it. The fish moves, I feel, uncertain what it is happening at first, but the tensing flyline focuses its mind, and the fish begins to use its weight to pull slowly. It feels heavy. Then its powerful body tries to take control, and it begins to run downstream. I have to use all my strength to turn its head so it will face upstream and be fighting both the current and myself. It doesn't want to oblige me, and I spot a rock just showing midstream – the fish is heading straight for it. No, no, no, I can't let it go around it – it would be a monumental fail – should it wrap itself around the rock I will lose it! A surge of adrenaline and I am bending the rod almost to destruction. It works, the fish starts to turn – it turns and I am in control, and although I ease off on the pressure, letting it have its head and run, I know it is beaten as long as I don't do anything silly. I am praying that none of the knots fail. I slowly bring it to the waiting net of a friend who is almost as excited as I am. We bring it to the bank and it is a hen fish of about 7lb. I would have liked to have recorded that it was a fresh-run salmon from the sea, a silver bar of a fish, but she had been in the river for some time and had lost some of her conditioning. Her flanks were not silvered but were showing a brownish tinge. We carefully unhook her and return her to the river. It might pass, this magical moment, but it is etched in my memory forever, and I feel elated.

There have been just a few occasions, I only realised retrospectively, when I have been what is called 'in the zone' when fishing. When you are 'in the zone' everything outside the present moment is banished and has no relevance over the intensity of the experience, with which you are now at one. Over twenty years ago a German-born resident of Canada, Eckhart Tolle, would describe how to attain this experience in his book *The Power of Now*, which pre-empted the recent mindfulness phenomenon by some years. The main theme of this book was that the only real thing that mattered was 'now' – by which he meant past and future were irrelevant. More than that, they hindered you from achieving fulfilment and happiness. Although I tend to agree with Will Storr in his book *Selfie* that it can be nearly impossible to change oneself or transcend the influence of your upbringing, *The Power of Now* encourages discarding the baggage of time past and time future by accepting and recognising the now. It is no surprise that Tolle was influenced by the Indian philosopher Jiddu Khristnamurti, whom I have written about in earlier chapters.

One of the tenets of Tolle's *The Power of Now* is the destructive nature of thought. "Not to be able to stop thinking is a dreadful affliction," states Tolle, "but we don't realise this because everybody is suffering from it, so it is considered normal. The incessant mental noise prevents you from finding that realm of inner stillness that is inseparable from being." He makes a distinction between consciousness and thinking, but "thinking is only a small aspect of consciousness. Thought cannot exist without consciousness, but consciousness does not need thought."

Similarly, Kristnamurti regards the treatment of thought as central to his philosophy:

> Why is there conflict between you, your husband or wife? In that relationship, thought plays a great part. Thought creates the image of the man or woman, and the relationship is between images. So actual relationship doesn't exist; it exists between these two images thought has created. So thought may be responsible for conflict. [...] You see very clearly that thought begins the mess in a relationship and then the question arises: how am I to stop thought? This is the wrong question because you, who wants to stop thought, are created by thought. So thought has divided itself as the controller and the controlled.

Eckhart Tolle was born in Luden, Germany in 1948. He described his childhood as unhappy. Growing up in post-war Germany, his playground consisted of bombed-out buildings. After his parents separated, he moved to Spain with his father. At nineteen he moved to London and taught German and Spanish at a language school, then, in his early twenties, enrolled at the University of London to study Philosophy, Psychology and Literature. After graduating he was offered a scholarship to do post-graduate research at Cambridge University, but dropped out soon after starting, and instead stayed with friends or at a Buddhist monastery. When he was twenty-nine years old, suffering from depression that had dogged him throughout his life, he had a life-changing epiphany. He changed his first name (he was christened Ulrich), some say in homage to the German Philosopher and mystic, Meister Eckhart, and began working as a counsellor and spiritual teacher in Glastonbury. In 1995, he settled in Vancouver where he met his wife, Kim Eng. His first book, *The Power of Now*, was published in 1997. Only 3000 copies were printed, and he and his friends touted them around Vancouver bookshops. It began to sell and became a publishing sensation when it was republished by New World Library in 1999. A year later, it reached the New York Times bestseller list – after two years it reached Number 1, had been endorsed by Oprah Winfrey and translated into thirty-three languages. Further books published in 2003 and 2005 had similar success. In 2008, Tolle partnered with Oprah Winfrey to produce several webinars which gained an audience of eleven million viewers, and subsequently streamed monthly group meditations on his website. The *New York Times* called him the most popular spiritual author in the United States, and in September 2009 he attended the Vancouver Peace Summit as a speaker alongside the Dalai Lama. He produced DVDs which were sold commercially but, like Goenka before him, he has always been cautious about his organisation taking on the status of a 'cult' or a managed, commercial enterprise.

My business partner and I developed a business that, because of its success, allowed us both to retire relatively young. I think I would have benefited then from the lessons in *The Power of Now* about how we interpret time, but didn't read it until some years later. I was Administration and Financial Director, and although not visiting the past much, I never really lived in the present either. I excluded 'past and present' because what could happen, what could affect our business, was based solely in the future. I walked around oblivious of what was happening day-to-day, apart from reviewing immediate financial data, with not much more in my head than: where do we go from here, what do we have to do, how do we stay a step ahead of our competitors? What about when I wasn't working? Well, nothing really changed. Because I have a somewhat obsessive personality, I couldn't switch off from work mode, so family life was tolerated rather than enjoyed. Christmas would come and go with just the two days off – I prepared for the end of year accounts, taking a literal view that everything had to be completed by the end of the year, which was of course, nonsense; our accountant wouldn't ask for them until Spring. I liked the word 'ramification' and used it a lot – 'the possible result of a decision or action' but being a procrastinator too meant that, well, more time than ever was spent looking to the future. My wife took me to the Maldives a few days after I retired, which was a very good move, and helped me to disconnect from my life in the company: my past life.

The Power of Now was a revelation when I read it, but I don't know whether I would have adapted myself to its teachings whilst working. I will never know, but it showed me an alternative conception of time, and how only the 'now' mattered – how easy it is to become fixated with our past and future selves. Eckhart Tolle wasn't the first to acknowledge that we all have incessant, compulsive thoughts and inane chatter that takes place inside our heads, but he identified that most of these thoughts are anchored in the past or future. He writes that a person who verbalises them is regarded as slightly mad, but the only difference really is that a 'sane person' won't say them out loud but will still allow them to occur inside their heads. Involuntary or compulsive thinking isn't always relevant to the situation you are experiencing at the time, but usually references something that has happened in the past or something that might occur in the future. In acknowledging that it is impossible to stop such thoughts, Tolle advocates being a witness of the thought, watching it and not judging it. You achieve a presence, separate from your mind, described as a 'watching consciousness'. Another way to do this is by intensely focusing all your senses on the present, the now. By using these methods it is possible to banish thoughts of the past and future that overrule your mind.

Why does the mind dwell on things other than the present? Eckhart Tolle says that this is because the egoic mind cannot function and remain in control without time. To ensure that it remains in control, it seeks to continuously cover up the present moment with past and future. Time isn't precious, it is an illusion. What is precious doesn't exist in time: the more we focus on past and future, the more the now is missed. So a dysfunctional mind operates only on the level of past and future, and I think we all suffer from this to some extent. There is also within us what Tolle describes as a 'pain body' that relates to past negative experiences, and leaves us with a residue and anticipation of pain. For some people this can take over their life, and Eckhart Tolle suggests that becoming the watcher of your emotions and thoughts can overcome the 'pain-body' within you. In some cases, the 'pain-body' is so powerful that it is part of a person's identity, and although they might deny that this is so, they would not wish it to go away! We might say "He's never happy unless he is miserable" — maybe that is an insightful observation of a person's 'pain body'?

The rare ability to be in 'the now' (if you can achieve it) is the acceptance of what is 'the now' and thought such as a hedonistic one, a thought that would necessarily incorporate something past or future will cancel out any attempt to achieve this 'now' mindset. Without thought, Tolle recognises, we would not be able to function, but it is the excessive thoughts that constantly bombard us that, he teaches us, is most destructive to our lives. But living in the present, in this time of Covid and its constraints, it is only too easy to reflect on what has happened or what may happen so we can easily find ourselves locked into the past/future conundrum. In the days of lockdown, it has been more important to try and practice the non-thinking 'now' accepting what 'is' but this is by no means an easy thing to do.

How has *The Power of Now* influenced my own life? I am more aware of dysfunctional thinking, but I can't say I am no longer prone to thoughts that have their heart only in the past or future. However, I am sometimes aware (when I remember) that there is another and more beneficial way of thinking. I am not able – and I have tried – to adopt a lifestyle of living solely in the now, and I don't think that is possible for most people, but when I remember and use the lessons drawn from Tolle's work, they have been helpful to me.

No other fish I catch will ever match catching the salmon – this King of Fish. But there is a sense of sadness too, because the decline of all salmon species throughout the world threatens them with extinction. Salmon are disappearing at an alarming rate, as a result of that all too common phrase 'a perfect storm' of circumstances. Once salmon feeding grounds were discovered off Greenland and the Faroe Islands, they were opened up to commercial fishermen, and drift netting commenced. Following a series of record annual catches, their numbers crashed between 1979 and 1990. Global warming has increased sea temperatures, affecting the food chain, particularly capelin, a major food source for salmon. In the sea lochs of Norway and Scotland, commercial fish farms have sprung up, supplying salmon for the table, but this has increased the amount of sea lice in wild stocks to detrimental effect. Farmed salmon that escape and breed with their wild cousins have reduced the genetic diversity of wild salmon, and furthered their decline. Rivers, the nurseries of the young salmon, now have doubtful water quality, and manmade barriers restrict salmon migration runs, making it harder for them to reach the place of their birth, including dams built to supply electricity, such as that on the river Beauly, the site of my first catch. Efforts have been made to ensure the salmon can circumvent these barriers, but dams still present a substantial obstacle to the breeding of wild salmon, and 2018 was the worst year ever recorded for salmon numbers. A survey found two-thirds of young salmon in the early stages of their migration to the sea perish, and only 5% now survive to return to spawn. Other estimates are as low as 1%. It isn't illegal to fish for salmon, but most water authorities insist right-fully that if you are lucky enough to catch one, they should be returned to the water. It is a very sad story for the King of Fish – there is no other fish like it, and that enshrines its natural beauty. One day, when the folly of man has led to our extinction, maybe a salmon will come to challenge Miss Ballantine's record catch in 1922, but there will be no-one left to see it.

Scotland is a staggeringly beautiful country but, as no-one would deny who has visited Scotland regularly, it is a very wet place. This doesn't really bother fishermen, although we would prefer it to be otherwise — we wear appropriate clothing. It doesn't bother the fish very much either, but after about five visits to my sister in Edinburgh over some years, the rain has dampened any desire that my spouse might have to revisit as a tourist, even for a short visit to the Trossachs one year in milder rain. So I go there with my fishing compatriots. On our last day in Inverness-shire we visited Glen Strathfarrar. Not open to the public, access is gained by obtaining a key to the locked gate. It was once Fraser country, before the Frasers forfeited the land, having been on the wrong side at the Battle of Culloden. Containing parts of the old Caledonian forest of Scots pine, it is home to Scottish crossbills, a type of finch, capercaillie, sika, roe, red deer and golden eagles. The scenery is breathtaking, even in a typical Scottish drizzle. When we visited, flora were ablaze with a brilliance of autumnal reds, greens and yellows. We stopped driving at the top of a hill and looked down on the loch, shrouded in mist. We glimpsed some small islands with little groupings of Scots pine and incongruous birch marooned on them. Further along, on a small hill, we came to a lone Scots pine that we were told was called Pauline's tree. A partner of someone called Pauline had laid her ashes there, and there is a plastic box with a pen and a note that begins 'a beautiful spot to rest' and invites visitors to comment on the view and their day. We didn't go up to Pauline's tree as we hadn't the appropriate footwear to encounter the boggy moorland. As we reached Loch Monar, ringed by the Munro peaks, we heard the loud bellowing of stags, eager to announce their participation in the rut, so we turned back.

Our last evening in the pub in the small village of Struy, we talked about our week as we ate our last meal. I was one of two in the group of six who had managed to catch salmon, and even though I had caught mine two days ago, I was still feeling the high. I paid for a round of drinks the night I caught it, but no-one likes to be reminded that they hadn't caught themselves, and as is the default mode when talk is about your own success, conversation veered towards other topics. It is a truism that everyone has to catch fish for it to be a good fishing day. This did not stop an attempt to sample every whisky from the optics that stretched across the length of the bar, with names unfamiliar to us from south of the border. We never managed to taste them all, to reach the last optic and the end of them, but most memorable was a measure of seventy-year-old Teachers that cost £35, and which we clubbed together so we could have a taste. It wasn't bad.

We left the next morning, after a breakfast of chanterelle mushrooms freshly gathered from the woods surrounding our cabins, which had been built from giant cedarwood logs imported from British Columbia, and we managed to join an army convoy that stretched for thirty miles along the A9. Although this would slow our journey up, and we had over 500 miles to travel, none of us were in a hurry to end that week-long fishing experience in Scotland, with its many highs. We would miss every moment and talk with some affection about this trip in future times.

| 6 |

New Zealand and the Klinkhamer

Klinkhamer

In early February, on a beautiful summer day far removed from the dismal weather we had left behind, we arrived on the South Island of New Zealand. In the UK I had had all our fishing tackle cleaned and sterilised by a vets practice, as the New Zealand authorities were fighting an invasive species which was having a notable impact on aquatic insects, a major source of food for many types of fish. This species was a diatom called alga didymo, that produced massive algal blooms and made riverbeds slippery for wading fishermen. Its insidious progress had already invaded many rivers on the South Island. All fishing tackle, they insisted, must be cleaned and thoroughly dried, and wading boots had to have rubber soles. Felt soles, if damp, could allow further proliferation. All our fishing tackle was inspected and got the OK.

I won't forget my first visit to the South Island of New Zealand. One third larger than the North Island, with a population of just over a million, and 40% living in Christchurch, the countryside is pretty much empty, save for the tourists. There are still regions that barely register one person per square kilometre. Tourists come for many reasons – we had come for the fishing – while others come for the multiple outdoor activities in a country so diverse it has glaciers, mountains, sub-tropical beaches and temperate rainforests. The South Island is remarkable for all this, but I loved it for being so empty. I would have gladly emigrated, except my partner, with inordinate common sense, wouldn't abandon a life made some eleven thousand miles away in the UK. It was a hopeless, selfish idea: why would she leave everything behind so that I could go fishing?

We had come to fish the Owen River, a tributary of the Buller, a short river that had a good head of brown trout averaging two kilos, but with much larger specimens. These fish were not going to be easy to catch, as they were easily spooked, so the difficulty quotient was high. Our guide for three weeks, Tim Tollett, though we didn't know it then, would put us through a sort of instructional course, verging on a masterclass, on how to fish this river. Tim was an American from Montana who ran his own guiding company on the rivers in his home country. He grew up on a cattle ranch and was introduced to fly fishing by his dad whilst young. He soon became an accomplished fly-tyer, selling them commercially only six years later. In 1977 he started guiding for well-known American fisherman Al Troth on the Beaverhead and Big Hole Rivers in Montana. Three years later, together with his wife Teresa, he opened Frontier Anglers, which has become one of the largest fly and fishing tackle shops in the US. As well as fishing and guiding in the Western states of the US, Tim has also guided and fished in some of the world's finest fishing waters, from Alaska to Belize, New Zealand, Chile, the Bahamas, Argentina and Canada. He has guided many famous people, including President Jimmy Carter. His quarry was all species of trout, salmon and bonefish, a saltwater fish of prodigious fighting ability.

Our party had some expert fly fishermen – I would class some of them as world-class, though that distinction didn't include me. Though I had fished with world fly fishing champions, Tim had to be the best fly fisherman I had ever met. I had come across him the day before, when I was trying to navigate through bushes and trees to another fishing spot where the river had split into two streams, and he fished as well as guided. He held his hand up, signalling me to keep down, and indicated that over the other side of an overgrown bush was a fat brown trout taking small dries. I thought "there's one trout that isn't going to feel a fisherman's hook!" Tim had other ideas. He somehow managed, through a tangle of branches, to get his fly onto the water, and it was taken confidently – then ejected quickly by the fish as Tim didn't lift the rod to set the hook. He couldn't: it was impossible to land the fish there, and the barbless hook caused no distress as it pinged into the bush. Why had he even attempted such an impossible feat? To see if he could deceive and fool the fish into taking his fly, knowing success was limited to the taking of his fly by the trout – that was all he hoped to achieve, and I knew of no fisherman other than Tim who would have tried it, or had the necessary skills. On another occasion I watched him cast into the teeth of a gale, then he coached me into having a go: reduce the nylon monofilament leader to two feet from ten feet, and cast, bringing the rod down as low as possible, almost to the ground. I tried and it was impossible, I couldn't do what he made look so easy and effortless. The wall of wind in front of me was so strong that it just dumped my flyline back to me. I made no progress and gave up.

Tim was a purist, a fisherman who eschewed competition fishing (all of us had done it) and the question of who could catch the most fish. He couldn't understand that his philosophy of 'man versus fish' could be reconciled with 'man versus man versus fish'. It didn't sit well with him, but he didn't show it. After all, he was in our employ as a guide, and we didn't mention it too much either. He had become a superb fisherman without having to prove himself to other fishermen.

We were on a low bank, and upstream, some 15-20 yards away, trout were rising on the Owen River where it disappeared into a left-hand bend. Tim, my buddy, and I were in a small clearing, keeping out of sight. Tim informed us that we had no more than two or three casts to these fish before they would become spooked and disappear. If we lined them with our flyline, then it was all over. We had already taken off the many dangly shiny bits that hung from our fishing vests: scissors, clippers etc, which might flash and announce our presence. Anything else was covered with a mixture of Fullers Earth and glycerin, a kind of glutinous mud smeared liberally over anything that might reflect glare. Flyline had been stripped off the reel and lay amongst the grass. It would be a problem if, when casting the line, it became trapped in the long grass and impeded the line from shooting through the rod rings. Tim produced a large pair of scissors and trimmed the grass enough for the flyline to lie flat on the ground. This was our 'casting platform'.

With great good nature, my buddy indicated that I could have the first go at casting to these fish, knowing I might well cock it up, blowing any chance he had of having a go at them. Trout didn't get to be the size they were on the Owen River without fear of predation – all wild fish had to have that to an extent, but angling pressure here had made them easily spooked. A sloppy, inaccurate cast and both our chances would have evaporated. My fly, a dry, was called a Klinkhamer, green and small, and was the invention of Hans Van Klinken, a Dutchman, in 1984. It became so popular that fish hook manufacturers now make a special hook on which to tie the fly.

Hans Van Klinken, born in 1956, lives in Holland, and began bait fishing when he was six years old. When he was thirteen he caught his first salmon in Norway, and at fifteen was using his father's cane rod to catch Arctic char and salmon. A year later, he was travelling alone to fish in Scandinavia. A little older, he visited the wilderness in northern

Lapland for four months, taught survival techniques by an old Sami (a native of Lapland) communicating only with him by hands and feet. He is quoted as saying that it was his greatest outdoor experience. When he could, he spent most of his schoolboy years in Norway, Sweden and Finland. He took up fly tying a few years later and invented the Klinkhamer, which proved successful when he started fishing with it in 1984. A modest man, he attributed his invention to others who had similar ideas at around the same time. In time, Hans became a fishing guide, writer, expert fly-tyer, and fisherman of salmon, sea-trout, brown trout and grayling. He also managed to squeeze in a career as a commander and gunnery instructor in the Dutch army, only retiring after 35 years. Since then, Hans has taken part in and organises programmes and workshops especially for children, offering youth an alternative to gaming and computers, trying to impart the importance of nature and wildlife to them, and the environmental issues that are more pressing than ever before.

There were trout rising about twenty yards away, and I could reach them with a reasonable cast of my flyline. If I cast twenty-one yards, I would line the fish, and they would scatter. I cast some yards short of the fish, then cast slightly longer to get a little nearer. My third cast landed in the correct area of the fish, but to the side, and it hadn't spooked them. My fourth cast was just right, and the response was immediate and violent, as a trout of maybe three kilos hit the Klinkhamer. It might have weighed more — I couldn't tell, as it was gone. It had broken my line and taken the fly, in what is known as a 'smash take' – an apt description.

A smash take occurs for various reasons, but the sheer power of a large trout is enough to explain it. I cursed; I wanted to catch that fish on this near impossible river, but at least I hadn't scattered the remaining fish. Trout do not exhibit some of the alarm signals of other fish species, such as changes in skin colour, but the act of diving for cover once they are released will be enough to signal to others in the vicinity 'there is danger here'. I handed the rod over to my pal. He could have a go at them. I do not know who coined the phrase 'the noble art of fly fishing' but I sure didn't feel it at that moment. Neither would one of old Isaaz Walton's sweet and honeyed phrases placate me. I had executed everything correctly to a disobliging fish.

I remembered that just a few years ago I had almost given up fly fishing, having read a book by a Buddhist monk called *The Mind and the Way*. The writer of the book, Ajahn Sumedho, became responsible for the land on which the Amaravati monastery was situated. He was approached by the local angling club and asked whether he would allow them to fish in a lake within the grounds. Sumedho accepted their claims that all fish would be returned unharmed, but he refused their request. He couldn't accept that the fish wouldn't in some way suffer from their capture. It was a powerful piece of writing, and at the time it profoundly influenced me in thinking of fish more as sentient beings. I considered giving up fishing. A tug of war with my conscience ensued, but I carried on fishing and am grateful that I did.

Ajahn Sumedho is an obscure writer, relatively unknown given the massive interest Western culture has generated in Buddhism in recent years. His book influenced me greatly at the time, not only with its insights into Buddhism, but the author's respect for all life. If I look back I should have, I suppose, also contemplated vegetarianism, but I didn't. I just felt that I should not terrorise an animal such as a fish. Sumedho is a monk and practitioner of the Thai forest tradition of Theravada Buddhism. Born Robert Karr Jackman in the US, he joined the Peace Corp in Borneo in 1964 and two years later, became a Buddhist monk and changed his name. For ten years he trained under his teacher Ajahn Chah, a renowned meditation master who encouraged him to go to the UK, where he became Abbot of the Amaravati Monastery in Hertfordshire. He remained there for 26 years, until his retirement in 2010. *The Mind and the Way* was his first book, with chapters on the four noble truths, the three refuges and the five precepts, and how they relate to the daily practice of Buddhism. It was the story of Sumedho and his journey that fascinated me: an American, born into a privileged society, struggling with a dogma quite alien to him and becoming a Bhikkhu, a Buddhist monk. In addition, the simplicity of his description of the four noble truths could not be classified as doctrinal Buddhism.

The first noble truth is that all beings experience suffering and pain. This is true even if one has led a privileged life, manifesting not only because of illness, ageing or inability to get what one wants or desires, but also perhaps as existential suffering. The second noble truth is that the cause of this suffering is craving, desire and attachment. The third noble truth is that eliminating craving, desire and attachment brings about the cessation of this suffering. The fourth noble truth is how this can be achieved, namely through the noble eight-fold path.

Why should we as Westerners concern ourselves with this? We are not Buddhist monks who have to adhere to and obey these truths. Neither are these teachings fundamental to us; we don't have to acquire the discipline necessary to the world of priests or monks. So we waver and think of other things instead of the four noble truths. It is almost like a diet; we know that following the rules will result in achieving our goals, but still, that chocolate bar is just too irresistible. Reflecting on the four noble truths might prompt you to revisit a time when you have expected, but not received, a material thing, or even received the wrong order at a café, and are chastened by having a negative reaction that you know is facile and petty – your craving for and attachment to something ordered and expected has led to this reaction.

Attachments such as your car, house, or your iPad are physical attachments, and becoming bereft when one of these is lost, stolen or taken away is the manifestation of these attachments. Attachments in the form of memories are frequent, but harder to pin down. I have often been motivated to meditate by remembering the state of sublimity I reached in an earlier meditation, desiring to replicate it. Invariably this prevents me from reaching that desired outcome – I have to go back to square one and accept that the past, and this attachment, cannot lead to a feeling of spiritual release. I am at my grumpiest when things do not go the way I expect them to go, because my expectations are closely allied to my attachments. Near the beginning of his book, Sumedho writes:

An understanding of the nature of suffering is an important insight. Now, contemplate this in your own experience of life. How much of your life is spent trying to avoid or get away from things that are unpleasant or unwanted? How much energy in our society is dedicated to happiness and pleasure, trying to get away from those unpleasant and unwanted things? We can have instant happiness, instant absorption, something we call non-suffering: excitement, romance, adventure, sensual pleasures, eating, listening to music, or whatever. But all this is an attempt to get away from our fears, discontent, anxiety and worry – things that haunt the unenlightened mind.

Sumedho writes constantly about the attachment and permanence that we crave. Seeking permanence is futile, because death is its inevitable enemy, yet attaching to things, whether mental or physical, is something we all do, myself included. I experience attachments on a personal level: isn't it normal to maintain attachments to our children, our spouses, our relatives? Yes, I think it is. But what if we heed the words of those such as Eckhart Tolle and Jiddu Khristnamurti, whose writings espouse concepts of impermanence and non-attachment? Sumedho writes that only by recognising and fully accepting non-attachment and impermanence in one's life, can one gain the freedom of eliminating the restrictions of a life lived through attachments. We are human beings, after all, subject to nature's laws. We are born, get sick and then die, and we have little to no control over this. Clinging on to attachments is a little absurd, he reasoned.

As I write this, the world is gripped by the Covid-19 pandemic, that began around the beginning of 2020, making the practice of non-attachment and impermanence more relevant than ever before. What had, for so long, been known as 'normal' and permanent, has been overturned, while the reality of our mortal impermanence feels closer still. We have been forced to really see and understand what it means for all things to be impermanent. However, this can also lead us to regard COVID, and all suffering, in the same way. That doesn't mean we should treat this subject lightly, we must treat it as seriously as we can, but by regarding something as impermanent, we can reduce, or at least understand the fragility of our attachment to it. The uncertainty that we experience in these grim times, and our fear that the change it will bring will be detrimental to us, is because we desire and expect permanence in our everyday lives. Non-attachment and recognising impermanence can therefore be an antidote to the fears caused by this pandemic.

At first I didn't really know what Buddhism was all about. It was a religion, I thought, and I wasn't into that. I had, and have, no interest in religion. Being brought up as a Catholic until my early teenage years, I began to realise that my instruction in Catholicism amounted to a kind of brainwashing, and I gave it up. I knew that religion of all kinds had fueled many conflicts, and Buddhism seemed to be somewhat exempt. Buddhists don't worship the Buddha as a god, but as a divine example of how to live by his teachings. It seemed to me that although it could be regarded as a self-help book, *The Mind and the Way* was more than that – it was a discourse on the philosophy inherent to the Buddhist religion.

Ajahn Sumedho writes in a very personal way. For instance, when trying to practice Metta (loving-kindness), he writes that he fell well short because he possessed a very jealous nature. If he became jealous of someone, he would try to subjugate those feelings, and instead go around deliberately praising that person, saying how wonderful they were. The trouble was, it soon became obvious that all this praise had a negative effect, and instead made his true feelings clear. Realising that he had to accept that he was a very jealous person, that this jealousy was something he couldn't control or influence, when these feelings were aroused, Sumedho would inwardly say, "oh jealousy, here we are again. Welcome jealousy. I am jealous because..." By accepting this part of himself, he was able to manage it.

I wish I was able to come to terms with what fishing is all about, and understand the many contradictions that continue after all these years to puzzle me. When I witnessed my partner catch a brown trout after I had passed the rod to him, I knew he was fortunate to have caught it. Twice he had lined fish with his casting, and yet amongst these difficult fish one had obliged him and taken his fly, and it was a specimen; colour, markings, fins and tail were all superb. I quickly took a photo of it. Back home, we reviewed the photos we had taken and amongst the many fine specimens, the Owen trout stood out. Shortly afterwards, and unsolicited, I received in the post a framed photo of the fish that Andrew had sent to myself and to others in the party, and to this day it is on my wall in my fly-tying room at home. There is a tiny part of me that begrudges others fish if I am fishless. I can't help it. I am subject to human frailties like Ajahn Sumedho, but I should have had that fish on the Owen River!

| 7 |

Richard Walker and the Red Sedge

Red Sedge

Fishing buddies have come and gone over the years – just as friends do – losing contact with some, moving away from others, and in some cases just developing different interests. The fishing is the glue when friendships last. Strategic friendships, in particular, are a vulnerable kind of friendship, cultivated for business reasons or for maintaining a relationship with other fishermen, for they only continue if beneficial to all parties. Nevertheless, a few of my fishermen friends do remain my friends, even if we have had some strong disagreements – mostly of a political nature – because they remain people I like and want to associate with (most of the time anyway). Two quotes I find particularly apt about friendship are from Somerset Maugham: "When you choose your friends, don't be short-changed by choosing personality over character", and Plutarch: "I don't need a friend who changes when I change and nods when I nod: my shadow does that much better". The continuation of friendships relies on maintaining regular contact, if not frequent: that contact can be occasional, and doesn't have to be time conscious or time-limited. At time of writing, the Covid pandemic has seemingly increased all contact with family and friends – our need to know how they are faring having a new urgency – and luckily for me, all is well.

Family members of course know you better than any friends – even long-term friends – can. When I was younger, I thought that friends were more important, but I now know that for me that isn't the case. One retains friendships by regular contact. Siblings, parents, aunts and uncles may not be in regular contact but when they are, a bond re-establishes itself, relaxing into conversations that are free-flowing and unstinted. Ralph Waldo Emerson's quote on friendship, "it is one of the blessings of friends that you can afford to be stupid with them", seems more applicable to family than friendship, to me at least. My family can know me so intimately as to never be surprised by any of my actions.

I met two of my buddies when I lived in Spain for a while. I met Ray in a coffee shop overlooking the beach of Playa Flamenca. He was a builder from Derbyshire and had lived in Spain for about five years already before I arrived. A fisherman of the lakes and rivers of Derbyshire, he missed those visits badly, and was re-energised by the news that there was a Spanish club that stocked rainbow trout in a lake just two hours away, near the town of Mula. I would regularly go to the UK in the summer to fish, but Ray hadn't wet a line for many years, and to my somewhat curmudgeonly friend in his fifties, this idea was like the arrival of Christmas to a ten-year-old. In a fishing tackle shop in Mula, armed with our N.I.E. Certificates – an official state form necessary to residing in Spain – our bank details, and our passports (I think Spain must be the red tape capital of the world), we approached a young man at the sales counter. "Hola," said Ray, then "pesca trucha association," (fish trout association), and the young man disappeared into the back of the shop.

"Well, that was good – what do we do now?" I said, after waiting what seemed an age. It wasn't entirely our fault that we never learned the lingo: our home, Costa Blanca, was one of the largest enclaves of British ex-pats in the world, and everybody, including the Spanish, spoke nothing but English. I tried to learn in the early days, but it was useless – I couldn't find anyone to practice on. Mula was different, a Spanish town that only used their native language. An older man appeared and, guessing we were not after fishing tackle when we answered only "nada" to his entreaties to purchase something, pointed to a poster we hadn't noticed that advertised the Mula fishing club. So we became members – but not before a visit to a notary solicitor, where our documents were inspected and then photocopied. It may have not been ideal – the fish, so evidently stockies, had stunted tails and fins, a poor substitute compared to the lakes back home – but we were pleased. This was a piece of a jigsaw that helped to make our Spanish sojourn complete, and our wives were glad to be rid of us and our grumbles about the lack of fishing. They still had to put up with the standard complaints, of course: fishing was no good because it was too wet, too sunny, too windy, too cold...

Much later, it was high summer, and I was boat fishing on Blagdon Lake with Ray, having persuaded him, on one of his rare visits to the UK, to come and fish with me. Blagdon is a 440-acre water in North Somerset. Construction was completed in 1905, and it is one of the oldest trout fisheries in England. Arriving at the timber-framed Grade 2 listed Lodge built in 1900, the sense of history is palpable, and thousands of anglers must share the reverence I have for this old building, on whose walls lie fat, monster trout in glass cases, engraved with the dates of their capture from times past. The lake lies in a valley on the edge of the Mendip hills, the village of Blagdon nestling above it.

We all have a special place. I learnt my fly fishing skills while fishing from Blagdon's banks so many years ago now. Ray has his: Ladybower Reservoir in the Derwent valley in Derbyshire. I didn't ask about the memories he had of the place. There was no need, because they would be much the same as mine, but no one could ignore the beauty that surrounded us where we were fishing that day. I have fished many lakes and reservoirs, but few compare with Blagdon, and I never tire of looking at its scenery. Being a native of the area, I could have chosen its larger sister lake, Chew Valley, but when I enquired at the fishing lodge and a Ranger told me that Chew Valley was performing better for fisherman than Blagdon, I would usually still opt for Blagdon, although my catch-rate wasn't so good. Fishing on Blagdon, it seemed to me, was hit and miss – either very good or hopeless, but the ranger had given me good news; it was fishing well.

I had talked so much about Blagdon to Ray that I knew his expectations were high. Most anglers soon learn, when fishing isn't good, to say "You should have been here yesterday," or "last week", "last month", "last year", then comes a grand story as to why. I was already preparing myself for this – we anglers have only ourselves to blame, because when talking up a fishing venue we always highlight red-letter days when the fishing was easy, we can't help it. Other anglers don't want to hear how hard a day you had, they have enough of them themselves, though tales of "the one that got away", which were usually true, resonated with every angler. I was guilty of hyping up Blagdon, and I knew Ray was charitable enough to cut me some slack, but I also knew that he was hoping some of my tales were true! Whenever we fish, hope rules over expectation, for if it was the other way around, we would soon suffer serious disappointments. Nevertheless, it is the host angler's duty to beef up his guest's belief in the water he is about to fish. Stories of previous successful days, though counter-productive, can sometimes be like the smell of freshly baked bread, producing the desired appetite – to go fishing!

The water had good visibility today – not suffering from algal bloom as it often does in high summer, which is caused by eutrophication. When an algal bloom has taken hold, I have sometimes dipped the end of my rod six inches into the water and not been able to see the end of it, and it is hopeless to expect to catch fish when they are unable even to see the fly. Brown blooms are the worst; you do stand a chance with a green bloom, but not much. We motored through the weed beds that were now dying back, and entered Butcombe Bay along the Butcombe shoreline, to the point where the bay narrows. We headed to the weed beds that almost quartered the bay, but one side was weed-free. We crept slowly so weed beds were at the back and on both sides, but the water in front of us was open. Quietly, we released the anchor and set up our rods. Three flies on a leader would be a standard 'rig', but with a lot of weed about, it courted disaster. When a fish is hooked and in-variably runs, there is a good chance of one of the other flies careering through the water and snagging on a piece of weed – then, unable to control events, and having to exert pressure to release the line from the weed, you invariably lose the fish. I chanced my arm and started with a two-fly setup, with a black buzzer on a medium-weight hook and a green one on a lightweight hook six feet away, so both fished at different depths.

Blagdon isn't particularly known for rising fish until later in the day, and none were showing themselves: nymphs were the best option and they worked. We probably caught about a dozen rainbows – none under 2lb and several over 3lb – and had fabulous sport, but our success was our downfall – it meant that we would have to move. By releasing these fish in a comparatively small area of water, we were sending alarm signals to the remaining fish, and after a half-hearted pluck at one of Ray's flies in the last hour we motored away. Ray understand-ably wanted to fish until the fishing day ended, and I knew it was going to be a long one. With a regular fishing partner on Blagdon, I would fish until about 5pm. If Blagdon proved bountiful, we would feel that our fishing day was complete; we were not fishmongers. If the fishing was tough or non-existent, then we knew there would be no improvement staying any later, and 5pm seemed a good time to quit. But today Blagdon wouldn't be rid of us until near 10pm, one hour after sunset and the official closing time. Reminiscing, drinking wine, eating and "just a few more fish" seemed to be the way we were going to end the day, and we were content with that. But it was early evening, and we were just off the bank at Ashtrees. The raucous noise of coots, feeding near the receding weed beds close by, split the silence, increased by the sounding-board effects of the calm lake. To our right was an area named Orchard Bay, and to our left, Peg's point, itself a hotspot for bank fishermen. With a slight ripple pushing us out into the open water, the sedges started to rise.

The aquatic sedge fly family belong to a group known as Trichoptera, with three life stages: the bottom-dwelling larvae, or grubs, build over themselves a protective camouflage of pebbles, small sticks, leaves and anything else lying about on the lake floor, then the pupae grow strong paddling legs and move fast through the water. Finally, at the surface, the thorax splits, and they emerge as moth-like adults with their wings folded to form a roof or tent shape. Now these adults were emerging in significant numbers, and we switched to dry fly techniques. I tied two size 12 green Klinkhamers onto my leader, ignoring the Red Sedge patterns that were more appropriate, given that they were a better match to the flies that were emerging – they were amongst my favourite, and logic sometimes lets you down. Ray, I think, tied on something similar.

Richard Walker, inventor of the Red Sedge, was one of the most influential anglers of the twentieth century. He was born in Hitchin, Hertforshire in 1918, educated at Friends School, Saffron Walden, and St Christopher School, Letchworth, then entered Gonville and Caius College Cambridge to read engineering. At the onset of World War Two he started working at the royal aircraft establishment, Farnborough, where he applied his knowledge of electronics and radio to play a prominent role in the development of radar technology. He started fishing at the age of four with his grandfather and became an accomplished angler, but he was to become more than that. He brought a scientific approach to the sport, hitherto bound by obfuscation and dogma inherited from the past. His inventions include the Arlesly Bomb, a pear-shaped weight useful in coarse fishing, the electronic bite indicator, and he was instrumental in the development of carbon fibre rods. Making split cane rods in his workshop, his MK IV Carp rod today fetches many thousands of pounds at auction.

Walker was a prolific writer for the angling press. His first article on fishing appeared in his school magazine, he went on to write a weekly column in the *Angling Times* for 30 years, and contributed articles to monthly magazines such as *Trout and Salmon*. His many books encompass both general and specific issues relating to coarse and game fishing. In 1952, at Redmire Pool in Herefordshire, he caught what was then the record carp - it weighed 44lb and took his bread paste bait on a 12lb breaking strain line. After a brief but eventful fight, a fellow angler netted the fish. Richard Walker knew this capture of his fish gave him the British and Commonwealth carp record, but if he returned it, it would just be another fisherman's tale. Walker contacted London Zoo, who immediately dispatched a van. The fish was transported to the aquarium, arriving there some 21 hours after its capture, but still alive. The carp, named Clarissa, lived for another 20 years and millions went to see her in her new home. Walker's record lasted for 28 years, until 1980, when a carp of 51lb 8oz was caught by Chris Yates, an angler of some repute, at Redmire Pool – the very same fishery where Richard Walker had caught Clarissa.

Growing older, Walker favoured trout fishing. With the opening of Grafham Water, then the largest man-made water in England, he concentrated on addressing the problems facing fly fishermen on this massive water, and developed many reservoir fly patterns, (including the Red Sedge) popularising them in his monthly articles in *Trout and Salmon* and his published book on fly-dressing innovations. His later years were marred by cancer, and he died in 1985. A remarkable man.

The fishing conditions were perfect, then they weren't. The wind suddenly died – not unusual on water in the evening and we were becalmed. That didn't stop the trout rising to the sedges, but it made casting to them more difficult because the lack of wind didn't help– the nylon leader wouldn't 'turn over' properly, and landed on the water all bunched up. It is possible to compensate by double-hauling (a casting technique) more vigorously to increase the line speed and therefore imparting more momentum, so that the leader and flies land in a straight line. However, unlike casting on a river, whose turbulent waters help to disguise the flyline, a flat calm exaggerates the flyline's presence, especially if you allow it to hit the glass-like appearance of the water too heavily. If this happens the fish will head for the depths, and your chances are ruined. If you are nymph fishing, you will usually have a heavier fly on the point of your nylon leader, which helps to improve your casting as it turns the leader over properly, but we were fishing dries. They were lightweight, and had to be so that they didn't sink. A slight breeze, then no breeze at all, the prospects of catching fish rose and fell. We floundered. Although the wine had long gone, its effects hadn't. Our casting was sloppy, and inevitably nylon leaders became tangled. We spent more time with our lines out of the water, untangling them, and the fish seemed to be mocking us as they rose closer and closer to our boat. They appeared to be saying here I am, here I am, before vanishing!

Then, a breeze – a breeze that began to move our boat over fresh water, over new rises, new fish – and the odds changed once again in our favour. Thoughts of heading for shore vanished. My hand hovered over the dry flies in my box. I saw the flies I had recently tied at my vice, took the Klinkhamers off, and tied on two small Red Sedge patterns, one on a dropper and one on the point of the leader. I realise now that I used the 'systems' Daniel Kahneman writes about so cleverly in his book *Thinking Fast and Slow*. At first I used the intuitive part of my brain to go for a fly that was a favourite of mine (System 1), but the rational, thinking part of my brain in the end overrode this, and chose the sedge fly copy (System 2). Nothing is quite what it seems in this book – neither system is better than the other, both can be wrong or effective.

I read *Thinking Fast and Slow* some years ago when it was first published. It is a remarkable book, the result of a collaboration over many years between two friends, Daniel Kahneman and Amos Tversky. A reviewer wrote that these were "two men who changed how people think about how people think", which is an apt description. Daniel Kahneman was born in Tel Aviv in 1934. Amos Tversky was borne in Haifa in 1937. Kahneman had a traumatic childhood, as his family lived in Paris during the Nazi occupation and, as Jews, were under an enormous threat. Kahneman's father was arrested, but released due to the intervention of his employer, Eugene Schueller, the founder of L'Oreal. They were on the run for rest of the war, but all survived, save his father who tragically died in 1944 due to untreated diabetes. They moved to Palestine in 1948, just before the creation of Israel. Kahneman received a bachelor's degree in Psychology from the Hebrew University of Jerusalem in 1954. What followed was a distinguished academic career of immense proportions: Lecturer in Cognitive Psychology at Harvard, Professor of Psychology at the Hebrew University of Jerusalem, the University of British Columbia and University of California, Berkeley, alongside numerous honorary degrees from other universities. He is currently the Emeritus Professor of Psychology and Public Affairs at Princeton. Then there are the enormous number of awards received throughout his lifetime, including the Nobel Prize for Economics – despite never having taken a single economic course.

Amos Tversky would have been co-recipient of the Nobel, but he died just six years earlier. The two men had little in common other than they were both rising stars in the psychology department at the Hebrew University of Jerusalem. Tversky had a less traumatic time growing up: he enlisted in the military and became a paratrooper, serving during the Suez crisis and the six-day war in 1967, and was decorated for bravery. He was always an optimist and said that it suited him because, as he put it, "when you are a pessimist and bad things happen, you live it twice, once when you worry about it and the second time when it happens". Kahneman, on the other hand, was a pessimist, claiming that "by expecting the worst, he was never disappointed."

In the late 1960s a partnership and a deep friendship began between them that lasted many years. Collaborations rarely last, though some produce work of merit, but theirs managed to radically change existing dogma and mindsets. They explored cognitive illusions that affect human judgment, and the continual biases and failures in rationality we exhibit in decision-making. As well as the Hebrew University of Jerusalem, Tversky worked at the University of Michigan before joining Stanford University in 1978, where he remained for the rest of his career. Like Kahneman, he was presented with many prestigious awards. He died of metastatic melanoma in 1996.

Thinking Fast and Slow was published in 2011, 15 years after Tversky's death, but developed during their partnership. The central thesis of the book is a dichotomy between two modes of thought and the cognitive biases associated with each type. System 1 is fast, instinctive, emotional thinking, while System 2 is slower, more deliberate, and more logical.

Kahneman illustrates these Systems with a puzzle:

A bat and ball cost £1.10. The bat costs one pound more than the ball. How much does the ball cost? A number came to your mind. The number, of course, is 10: 10p. The distinctive mark of this easy puzzle is that it evokes an answer that is intuitive, appealing and wrong. If you do the math, you will see. If the ball costs 10p then the total cost will be £1.20 (10p for the ball and £1.10 for the bat) not £1.10. The correct answer is 5p.

Well, when I read this puzzle years ago, it took me some time to understand it. Even reading it again now, I still have trouble grasping it. There is a kind of denial going on about the correct answer, which I know to be 5p, but it seems the intuitive part of my brain wants to ignore it. If this example proves intuitive thinking untrustworthy, then it also casts doubt on other thoughts produced by intuition. Kahneman says that "many people are overconfident, prone to place too much faith in their intuitions. They apparently find cognitive effort at least mildly unpleasant and avoid it as much as possible." Yet he still credits System 1, the intuitive system, with being more right than wrong: System 2 can become so overloaded with information that it cannot process properly, whilst System 1 cuts out the chaff to (sometimes) reveal a correct assumption. I can relate to this – often in my life I have tended to overthink something and, in the end, prove my intuitive instincts more relevant to the final decision.

Kahneman quotes a famous study where viewers were instructed to watch a video of a basketball match, with one team wearing white and the other black. They are instructed to ignore the black team and count how many passes were made by the white team, requiring intense focus. Halfway through, a woman wearing a gorilla suit appears, crosses the court, thumps her chest and moves on. She is on screen for nine seconds. About half of the viewers do not notice her – the result of a blindness caused by the counting task and instructions to ignore the black team. Not only this, but viewers who fail to see the woman dressed as a gorilla are also convinced that she didn't appear, and have to see the video again for proof she did. It illustrates two important facts about our minds; we can be blind to the obvious and we are also blind to our blindness. *Thinking Fast and Slow* isn't an easy book to just dip into; its target readers were meant, I think, to be those reading specialist journals on human psychology; but it still managed to sell one million copies in the first year, reaching the *New York Times* bestseller list.

Kahneman also researched hedonic psychology, the study of what makes experiences pleasant or unpleasant. He concluded that "remembered well-being" and "experienced well-being" diverge. The "remembering self" does not care about duration. We retrospectively rate an experience not by its peak level of pain or pleasure, but instead by the level of pleasure or pain at the end of the experience. He illustrates this with an experiment, not wholly ethical, in which two groups of patients undergo painful colonoscopies. The patients in Group A undergo a normal procedure. The patients in Group B undergo the same painful procedure, except with few extra minutes of less painful, mild discomfort at the end. When asked to state their level of pain, Group B patients, enduring the same pain as those in Group A and then some, felt they had suffered less. By prolonging their procedure, but ending it less painfully, their suffering had arguably been greater in the moment, but they remembered it as much less so. Their over-all experience was less painful because the mild discomfort at the end of their colonoscopy was key to remembering the total experience as a less painful – they seized upon this remembrance as accurate, even though their procedure had lasted longer. Group A had experienced pain without the conclusion of mild discomfort, and reported a more painful examination. He concludes that it is the remembering self that calls the shots, not the experiencing self.

A similar conundrum arises when we consult memories of personal experiences, as many psychologists and neuroscientists know. Memory is selective, adaptive, and sometimes unreliable. The day on Blagdon with Ray, if he were to recall it, I'm sure would differ from my recol-lection, although we would have had the same experiences. We might know what the weather was like, how many fish we caught and the flies we used, but nuances would abound in terms of how this related to us; how it affected us personally, emotionally. When friends fish to-gether you must both catch fish to make it a good day. Fortunately, we were both landing fish, although I had crept ahead on dries and the Red Sedge (you keep a tally of how many you have caught, without men-tioning it – we are after all a competitive species). I was skittering my flies across the surface, inducing 'takes', whilst Ray was content to let his flies remain static. We were both hitting some fish, missing others, due to an excess of adrenaline. We were all fired up as only dry fly fish-ing can make you. Sometimes this means you can be too quick to set the hook; the trout hasn't had enough time to take the hook properly, and you whip it out of its mouth. This, of course, you attribute to the trout missing the fly – heaven forbid it was anything but the trout's fault!

With the light failing, I had a two fish hookup, in which both dry flies had fish on them at the same time. This occurred when fishing with nymphs sub-surface, but never when I fished dry flies. It isn't a good thing when this happens, as the outcome is uncertain. When trying to catch fully-fit fighting rainbows, you are rarely able to land both: with both fish pulling in opposite directions, the strain on knots and nylon is just too great, and consider yourself lucky to land one of them. Usually I find that the fish on the 6" dropper, perpendicular to the main leader, will break free, then there is a chance of netting the fish on the point fly. Today, this pattern was reversed: I had lost the fish on the point, and the fish on the dropper fly was now giving me an aerobatic display, jumping four feet out of the water. I managed to land it, and was grateful that the gods had looked favourably on me. Our time was up on Blagdon, and we had had a marvellous day's fishing. You can never have a bad day on Blagdon. You might not catch any fish, but it is always a good day.

| 8 |

Chew Valley Lake and a forgotten fly

Black Pennell

Chew Valley Lake is a large reservoir created to supply Bristol and the surrounding area. It obtains its waters from the Mendip Hills and, with a surface area of 1200 acres, is the fifth largest artificial lake in the UK. It was designated an area of outstanding natural beauty and, prior to the flooding that created the reservoir in 1956, archaeological excavations found evidence of people from the Stone, Iron and Bronze

Ages. It's a fishery where 260 bird species and 30 species of mammals have been recorded, and one I frequented often for many years, as I lived within twenty minutes of its shores. One late September day I was fishing on a boat with Roger, a friend from Spain.

Although Chew Valley Lake and Blagdon only have a few miles between them, they are very different. Chew is almost three times larger, and the flat expanse of water can be whipped up by the wind, producing some serious waves. There is little shelter except behind Denny Island, the only island on the lake. The fishing is different too: Chew seems to provide more free-rising fish during the daytime, whilst Blagdon has the edge on evening rises of fish. One can fish very well whilst the other languishes, and is next to being hopeless, but there is no contest when it comes to scenic beauty – Blagdon, smaller and nestling in a valley, is by far the prettiest. Although this phenomenon hasn't been seen for some years, Blagdon also features what is referred to as 'the Blagdon boil', when, approaching dusk, there are so many fish moving to trapped nymphs just under the surface that the whole lake seems to be boiling, like a pan of water on a stove.

Roger spent his summers in Derbyshire, away from the searing heat of Spain, and we had fished the Derbyshire waters – Carsington Reservoir, Rutland Water and Blithfield – together many times. We had always done well. This September he was staying at his son's house close to Chew, so we met and fished either Blagdon or Chew Valley. For the sheer beauty of its location, Blagdon was Roger's favourite lake, and we had fished it often, but today we were at Chew, on one of my home waters, and we were going to have a good day. Reports were abroad of good catches, and the weather was going to be fine. Perhaps it would have been better with a little more cloud to diffuse the sun's brightness on the water, but hey, can you call yourself truly committed if you always aspire to perfect fishing conditions? It would be good enough.

The buzzer hatches had gone. In early season the hatching insects are so dense that they appear as clouds over the bankside trees, but today none were visible. Some daddy longlegs had been blown over from the bankside onto the water, and that would interest some trout, but the main hatches wouldn't re-appear until the next spring.

Roger and I were drifting slowly in the boat from Moreton Bank. The vegetation was now dying away from its peak so we could get closer to the shoreline, and, as a friend used to say, "we were in the pound seats," meaning that this was where the fish were likely to be. Uttering obscenities unusual for this mild-mannered man, I saw Roger tying on another fly.

"What happened?" I asked.

"Just had a smash take". The fish had broken off the fly and swum away. I hadn't noticed, although I was only seven feet away at the other end of the boat, absorbed as I was in my own fishing.

Nylon monofilament, the material that makes up the 'cast', is strong and thin but deteriorates and weakens in ultraviolet light. Last year's spools are suspect. A smash take can be caused by other things – sometimes when too much wine has been drunk too early – but we hadn't reached that stage yet. There are also other reasons for smash takes, such as a failure of technique, but ten minutes later, when Roger was again tying another fly, I knew that faulty nylon was the culprit.

"I'm going up to 7lb breaking strain from a new spool I bought recently," he said. Chew trout are always a handful, and although I use a 5lb breaking strain cast (tying a 5lb weight onto this line, then trying to lift it, should break it) I could see the sense in increasing the breaking strain. It worked and he suffered no more smash takes that day.

Roger had fishing in his DNA. His father was a fisherman and as a child he used to take him sea fishing to the Isle of Grain, a desolate spot, as he said, "far removed from the radar of ice cream vans". He used lob worms to catch eels – although only his mother would eat them. The thread of fishing continued throughout his life to the present day: he was a natural and won many competitions and prizes in sea and coarse fishing. He only began fly fishing some eight years ago when, in me, he found a patient soul who could show him the ropes. Within a short time he could match his skills against most fly fishermen, and today he began to show me how it was done by catching two rainbow trout. "What are you catching on?" I said to my one-time pupil. He didn't answer straight away, occupied as he was in unhooking the trout he had just caught "on the point fly, which is a Black Pennell," came the reply.

Black Pennell... Black Pennell... God, I didn't have one of these in my fly boxes anymore. I had removed that fly some years ago, when I had decided it was surplus to requirements, and here it was, catching fish. My Crunchers and Diawl Bachs, different fly patterns usually so effective, weren't working – I would have to ask Roger for a loan.

It's a given that borrowing a fly results in you keeping it – you might tentatively volunteer to give it back, but no fisherman accepts that, in my experience. There are flies like the Black Pennell that, for no good reason, go out of fashion. One fly, the Alexandra, a heavily dressed wet fly of peacock eye and herl feathers, was so successful that some trout waters reportedly banned its use. Another, a fly called a Mallard and Claret, was often a top dropper fly favourite of mine, but, like the Black Pennell, somehow it was found wanting and replaced by... well, by whatever the fishing magazines were touting as the latest new wonder fish-catching cert. Roger handed over one of his Black Pennells and I tied it onto my cast.

The Black Pennell was invented by Henry Cholmondeley-Pennell (Cholmondeley, a mouthful if ever there was one, is pronounced 'Chumley'). Born in 1837 of rich parentage, he was privately tutored and lived in Chelsea and Palace Mansions in Kensington. He became a civil servant and, during his career, became HM Inspector of sea fisheries, eventually working for the Khedive of Egypt as director-general of interior commerce. Although little is recorded of his private life – he was married to Susan Avery, but it is not known if he had any children – we know he was a naturalist, poet, editor, author and fisherman. Most of his books, both of poems and about nature and fishing, are now out of print, and he never became one of those famous, prominent Victorians. As a naturalist, he published a book about whether fish feel pain; as a poet, several books of poetry. Although there is little evidence that he fished that often, or where he fished, he produced several books on the three branches of fishing, namely Sea, Course and Game fishing. He was an editor of *The Fisherman* and he also contributed to *Punch* magazine. In a review of Pennell's *The Classic Guide to Fly Fishing*, the writer Theodore Gordon, sometimes referred to as the father of American dry fly fishing, wrote "it is impossible to grow weary of a sport that is never the same on any two days of the year. It is this enthusiasm for the sport that H. Cholmondeley-Pennell, one of Britain's most famous nineteenth-century naturalists, conveys in this comprehensive guide to fly fishing, one of the very first 'manuals'."

Black flies have been around for centuries, and typically have drab colours that mimic the colouring of natural insects: greens, greys, sometimes black. Fly-tyers have used them through millennia. Black or dark colours shape the way an aquatic insect is profiled, so black is a natural choice. When Cholmondeley-Pennell added the tail of a golden pheasant tippet to what was a basic black fly, he created a fly like no other, one that then became a standard pattern through its success in catching trout. Some would say the Black Pennell wasn't all that different from any other black fly, but all new flies borrow from the past, and he revamped it in a way that deserved to have his name. Very few flies of the many thousands have been named after their creator. Those with flies to their name mostly belong to a bygone era. Flies are now named for many reasons, some of them whimsical, but not many today are named for their makers.

I don't have much of what I would call an educational background. I failed my 11plus (none of my siblings passed it, in fact) and started at a Catholic secondary modern school some miles away from the local school, which was nearer and it turns out a lot better. My school gave us a woeful educational experience in which we seemed to learn very little – every year we learnt just what we had learnt the previous year – so it seemed that nothing was newly learnt, just regurgitated. In my second year, Mickey Lloyd and I, with a sense of ennui about the whole process and a desire to be anywhere else, skipped school and played truant for six weeks. We spent the time behind the bus station next to the railway lines, and there met a dozen or so other runaways from our school, mostly older boys. I had my first puff of a cigarette. I was thirteen years old. Eventually I was caught, but their incompetence was my friend, as they had me recorded as missing school for just two weeks. I didn't enlighten them – they hadn't enlightened me! I returned, and no action was taken, no detention, no lectures. I left at fifteen, as most did, and few, if any, went on to further education. I became a warehouseman (or boy, as I wasn't a man) at a wool company supplying knitting wools.

Reading, however, left an indelible mark on me. It has always been a passion, along with my desire to find out what the world was about, what it offered me. Through books I began to understand that experiences of every possible nature were available, there in black and white, and formal schooling, which for me was non-existent, didn't matter. From my days reading *The Secret Seven, The Famous Five* and later the *Biggles* books, I moved onto the Russian authors Gogol and Dostoevsky, then the American heavyweights: Hemingway, Updike and Bellow. Before these, I was enraptured by science fiction, by the American author Ray Bradbury and his books *Fahrenheit 451* and *The Martian Chronicles*. I also had someone to talk to about them – my older brother, ten years my senior, who was a fan of Ray Bradbury. Returning home from a night on the town, quite late, Bernard (we always called him Bo) and I would discuss these marvellous books. For the first time I had another person who was experiencing the very things I was. Over the years I have read, I suspect, thousands of books: novels, travel books, books about science and philosophy, autobiographies – and forgotten most of them – but I remember the great ones, the ones that got under my skin, were revelatory, or were simply great works of fiction.

In the course of this reading, and the course of life in general, I have encountered many concepts that left me flummoxed and bemused. No matter how I struggle to understand them, there is no way – I haven't got the brains – but it would be nice to at least try to understand the big issues. I'm referring to the very small and the very big – Quantum Mechanics and particles like Quarks and Higgs bosons, astrophysics and astronomy with the very large galaxies and nebulae – their extremity seems preposterous, absurd – I cannot, however hard I try, have much of an understanding of these subjects. But another big concept does fascinate me, and I think I understand it more: consciousness. Consciousness allows me to be aware of what I cannot know, what I am not brainy enough to know, and what I do know. Growing older, coming through a difficult adolescence, introspection engendered in me an ability to examine the thoughts and ideas (from learned experiences mainly) that I knew were somewhere in my head: mind or brain, I supposed, but it didn't seem to be enough somehow. I wondered how thoughts made their largely unsolicited way into my consciousness, why they just appeared there. It was, for me, a small step from that point to asking just what consciousness was: what was, where was this enabling ether that engendered the thoughts that I encounter every day? But it was a much bigger step to try to pin it down. I became fascinated by the concept of consciousness. It seemed to me to be as mysterious as the dark matter that scientists talked about, that has been estimated to comprise as much as 85% of the mass of the universe and yet cannot be detected. Just what was consciousness, and where does it reside, if not in our brains?

I have long been fascinated with just where or how consciousness resides within us, one of the great unanswerable questions of our time. Schools of thought differ, neuroscientists disagree, and new theories abound. One such new theory is 'The Spread Mind', which I became aware of when reading a book by Tim Parks titled, appropriately, *Out of my Head*. The simplest explanation of consciousness is that it involves a subject knowing an object, but how can it be explained – what is it? This seems to most people to border on trivia, compared with their daily life experiences, and might meet a cry of 'who cares?' or 'so what?', but to those pursuing it, it is the holy grail. Artificial intelligence can beat us at chess, can predict the onset of cancer as well as human oncologists, and rout out financial fraud better than professional auditors, but has no consciousness, no awareness of itself. Consciousness is, at its simplest, "sentience or awareness of internal or external existence" – but this subject becomes as complicated as it is possible to get – even dictionary definitions of consciousness can produce a bout of head-scratching.

I have already mentioned Tim Parks, author of *Out of my Head*, in my account of pursuing the meditation technique of Vipassana after reading *Teach Us to Sit Still*. Parks was born in Manchester in 1954 and, having attended Cambridge and Harvard Universities, he moved to Italy, where he has remained for over thirty years. He taught translation as a university professor at the University of Milan, but somehow found the time to produce an enormous body of work since the publication of his first novel in 1985. Nineteen novels followed, earning him several literary prizes – his book *Europa* was shortlisted for the Booker Prize – then there are his fifteen books of non-fiction on a wide range of subjects, and seventeen translations of Italian works, including by Machiavelli, Leopardi and Calvino, receiving yet more prizes. The love of his adopted homeland has produced books about Italian neighbours, Italian education, Verona Football Club, and the Italian train system, and then feeling, I suppose, that he hadn't done quite enough, he penned articles for the *New Yorker*, the *London Review of Books* and the *New York Review of Books*.

Tim Parks had help – as he would be the first to acknowledge, a lot of help – from Riccardo Manzotti, the creator of 'the Spread Mind theory' that Parks so eloquently explains in *Out of my Head*. Manzotti has a PhD in robotics, degrees in philosophy and computer science, teaches psychology and perception at the University of Milan, and has been a visiting Fulbright Scholar at MIT. A few years ago, friends Parks and Manzotti had a series of discussions, driven by Manzotti's theories that I first read on Park's Facebook page, and which developed into fifteen dialogues of consciousness that, I believe, is now on YouTube. In 2017, Manzotti published his book *The Spread Mind Theory*.

So what is this all about? In discussions of consciousness, the 'internalist' view holds that everything, sight, taste, touch, smell, etc, is powered by neural activity alone – the brain, the mind, is all-powerful. The 'externalist' view is that the conscious mind is not only the result of what goes on in our brain, but also what occurs and exists outside of the brain. Externalists believe consciousness is not just of the brain or its functions. The Spread Mind theory is a theory of radical externalism, posited by Riccardo Manzotti, which Park's book explores in layman's terms. Manzotti explains:

> According to neuroscience, consciousness is secreted by the brain, much as the pancreas secretes insulin. We are told that information gets in, neurons do some magic and consciousness is excreted. So far, though, neuroscience has been unable to explain why neural firings should produce consciousness. As of yet, the world's greatest minds have not been able to outline a convincing explanation.

This seems a little complicated. Believing that consciousness happens inside our head is compelling from a human perspective and, as Parks puts it, "it is attractive to think of our mind, our experiences, as entirely ours, as separate from the world experienced". We haven't got very far in trying to pinpoint what part of the brain may be the source of consciousness, either. In an experiment by Professor Zeki, at which Parks was present, volunteers looked at conflicting images whilst wired up to sophisticated electrical equipment which mapped out the electrical responses in different areas of the volunteer's brain, whilst others tracked the results. Brain activity flicked backwards and forwards between two different areas of the brain. Voila. But Ron Chrisley, an expert in AI, wasn't impressed: "If you tell me which circuits of a computer are active when its chess program moves knight to queen's bishop 3, you really haven't told me very much about chess."

What about illusions, hallucinations, and dreams? These are explained counter-intuitively in mainstream thinking as unusual quirks in perception, mismatches and perceptual 'time' relationships. Manzotti argues that "one's consciousness is not what goes on inside one's brain, one's consciousness is the physical object one is conscious of". He tries to simplify this in his red apple experiment, where he introduces a red apple and asks if the red apple materialises magically in the grey mush of the brain, or in the neurons and synapses of the brain – no, he concludes, our consciousness is the red apple we experience. As Tim Parks explains; The mint we suck, its mintiness, is the object, our consciousness, it is not in our brain or anywhere else – another analogy by Manzotti – our consciousness is the mint and the mintiness that we experience. He explains that "Our consciousness of the world is the world we experience. Our mind is made of what lies outside our bodies. The spread mind is a physicalist theory – it suggests that the thing we are is physical, but it is not our body. By means of our bodies, the mind is a collection of objects producing a joint effect."

I see a connection between Manzotti's statement "I am not, now. I am now." and Eckhart Tolle, who entreats us to live only in this 'now'. Tolle believes that using the mind other than for practical purposes can have a detrimental effect, and that creativity is sourced, in particular, through a no-mind scenario. From his book *The Power of Now*:

> You can also create a gap in the mindstream simply by directing the focus of your attention into the Now. Just become intensely conscious of the present moment. This is a deeply satisfying thing to do. In this way, you draw consciousness away from mind activity and create a gap of no-mind in which you are highly alert and aware but not thinking.

It is strange that two people, working in completely different disciplines, namely philosophy and neuroscience, can view the 'now' and the whereabouts of mind-functionality so similarly. Maybe the search for consciousness is an unnecessary one and rather pointless because it works, it is always there (somewhere) and functions reliably. Then, if the mind can be found in the brain, what significance can be allotted to the hundreds of millions of neurons making up the enteric nervous system – the concept of a 'second' brain residing in the stomach – that gives us our 'gut instincts or gut feelings' that influence our decision making on a conscious level?

Roger and I, with our Black Pennells, had caught a few fish in the bay off Moreton bank, but our catch rate plummeted to zero, and it was time to try another area of the huge lake. There were few anglers out that day; other clustering boats wouldn't reveal the location of the fish to us, so I started the engine and moved slowly across the lake. It is sometimes fruitful to do this because you might spot some rising fish, which means you can demonstrate your dry fly fishing skills, but with few insects hatching that day, the surface water was only ruffled by the South-West breeze. It is always good to fish Chew, as there is freedom to fish anywhere. It is a water where most anglers allow their boats to drift, but unlike Chew, the majority of Blagdon boat anglers seem to opt for anchoring. This is frustrating for boats that want to drift. We can, if we are drifting, maintain the belief that in covering water, we cover fish, and cover fish that might be tempted by our flies. The alternative, anchoring, if time lapses with no 'takes' to the fly, that precious belief that there are fish in the vicinity evaporates, and with it the great motivational hope that keeps us fishing. Then again, drifting boats will pass over shoals of fish, missing them – perhaps picking up the occasional one – whereas a shoal might stay near an anchored boat for some time. Fishing then can be extremely productive. Drifting, on the move through ever-changing scenery and ambience, is preferable to me. In early season there is a fishing bonanza to be had, and Top End at Blagdon, a relatively small area, can contain up to twenty anchored boats. If you want to fish there, you have no choice but to anchor. At times I will anchor, which at lunchtimes allows you to sip your wine and eat your sandwiches and go for a wee – yes, peeing on the boat, into a container called a baler, is what anglers need to do – then it is emptied overboard. There is no other way!

On occasion I have discovered a 'pod' of fish whilst drifting on Blagdon, only to see the area containing this pod suddenly turn into a no-go area, as boats having seen me catch, anchor there and cut me off. There is a rule, though I'm not sure whether it is a written one, that boats should not anchor into other boats' drifts, but this is mostly ignored, and on Blagdon anchored boats are prevalent. You must accept this. Being 'cut-up' when driving, I might succumb to a bit of road rage, but here, on the water, it is harder, though safer, to confront the anglers who have strong-armed you away from the action and ignored the rules of boat etiquette. Sometimes, of course, this isn't blatant – just unthinking – at least I tell myself this, as I view fellow fishermen more kindly than my fellow man! Anyway, it is fruitless to remonstrate across stretches of water, where a lot would be lost in the translation. You have to come to terms with the fact that that this is how it is.

We had now motored and fished most areas of Chew and had no more success. There was a little colour in the water due to a late algal bloom. Cloud and a slight wind made for ideal fish-catching conditions, but we weren't catching trout. Motoring to the Dam area, I was beginning to accept that we might have to call it a day. With six fish to the boat, it would still be a good day's fishing. Then I saw that the aerators were on! Our prospects looked good. The aerators are powerful pumps that lie on the lake floor and release large amounts of oxygen which rise up to the surface, agitating and aerating an area of 10-15 meters diameter. The fish love them, for this action brings up from the depths aquatic nymphs and larvae to feast on. Spread over 70-80 acres, the water authorities switch on eight or ten of these aerators to control algal blooms when the water's oxygen content is low. With so many aerators, if you are not successful at one, or your catch-rate dries up, you can just go to another. At Bewl Water in Kent, I have heard the rangers describe their aerators as the 'children's playground', so it can be easy fishing.

However, the necessary skill for landing your fly into this maelstrom of water was to get the boat drift right, so that Roger and I could cast into this small area of agitated waters. I set up a drift 25-30 meters away from the aerator. If the wind remained stable, both of us would arrive at the lip of it and one would cast to the left, whilst the other would cast to the right, with an equal chance of hooking a fish. The powerful upwelling of water the aerator creates can push the boat to one side or the other of the maelstrom, and I wasn't getting the drift right. The wind, by veering just a few degrees, changes the course of the drift, making the boat shoot past the aerator. On those occasions at least one of us still had a chance to plant our flies into the killing zone, but the drift was happening to me too frequently. As the drift erred to my advantage I cast, catching fish, and the boat swung away from Roger. Roger is a laid-back sort, with a great deal of patience, but I guessed that he thought he was being handicapped – I think I would have thought the same – and I felt, unreasonably, a little guilty. Then the wind direction started to stabilise, and the drifts became truer. I consciously tried to compensate, so that he had a shot at the fish in his target area, and soon he started to catch. The fish we hooked fought as hard as any I could remember, jumping into the air, performing triple salchows, and tearing away at speed.

A problem arose of my own making, because I had left my landing net in my car, thinking that Roger's would suffice. Chances of both of us hooking fish at the same time were remote, and two landing nets in a boat that measured some twelve-foot from bow to stern would clutter up an already cluttered space. Now there was a shout of "got one," met with "so have I," and one net between us! You hope you can claim first use of it by bringing the fish close to the boat first, but my, those fish were not going to oblige, and it was an effort just to keep our fish away from each other – if lines and fish became entangled disaster would ensue. We got them in one by one, this double hook-up, then it happened again two drifts later! I succeeded in claiming the net first, my fish being smaller. We subdued eight of them on this one aerator in 90 minutes of high octane, adrenaline-filled, arm wearying and very special sport. I will not leave Black Pennells out of my fly box again!

At the car park, just about to leave, the scrawniest fox you are ever likely to see wandered to within fifteen meters of us. Starving, he looked balefully at us. We had immensely enjoyed another wonderful day's fishing, and did not need the trout we had hooked and returned – worlds away from this wild animal who scrapped for all it could eat, and was probably feeding a litter of cubs. The world we human beings had inherited seemed unfair, unbalanced. Roger had taken one fish, damaged by a pike on its flank, for his son's cats, and took pity, leaving the trout close enough for the fox to grab it and disappear. The fox probably is no stranger to the car park, and fishermen's trout!

| 9 |

Floating down the Beaverhead River

Elk Hair Caddis

Why did I become a competitive fly fisherman? In my mid-thirties I was a member of a club that entered teams into some big national competitions, so I guess having reached some competency, it seemed a natural thing to do. To the high priests of our sport, such as Frederick Halford, the father of the English dry fly tradition, or G.E.M Skues, the inventor of fly fishing with a nymph, competition angling must have been a complete anathema – a betrayal and wickedness that they would never condone. Old Isaac Walton would have regarded it as treason.

What is in no doubt about competitive fly fishermen is their single-mindedness in catching fish – the focus is always on the quantity that they can weigh in at the end of the competition – but what of all the dead fish? We rarely want them. We like to think that giving them away to be eaten is the answer, but, I think, many are binned – a sad ending for this beautiful creature. We are all fish-catchers, and I am no preacher as to which way we should all fish, but I think the fishing loses something when it is done competitively. The fisherman who enjoys being in a place of natural beauty with friends and companions, who can reflect on his day's fishing without the desire to bring in the biggest bag of fish, and who can release all he catches, is a fisherman I aspire to be! I do wonder now what my motives were in the six years of competition fishing, and I think, on reflection, it was just an ego thing. It made me a better fish-catcher but not necessarily a better fisher-man. It seems to me, in knowing this, something is awry, and affects our consensus of what fly fishing is, or should be, based on its long traditions. Competitive fly fishing, a relatively young development in the sport, impinges unfavourably on these traditions for me.

I was an average competitive fly fisherman. Sometimes admitting to being average isn't easy – for instance most drivers, when quizzed about their driving skills, will put themselves in the 'above average' category – but I had my good days as well as bad ones. I couldn't say I enjoyed it that much – after eight hours of intense concentration, my brain felt like mush. You go out in a boat with a member of a different team (teams are usually comprised of six people), and are never paired with a member of your own team. The man on the engine is 'Captain' for two hours, which puts him in charge of where to fish for that time. It then switches to the other angler, so every two hours, in theory, a new decision about where to go is made. However, it soon becomes obvious where to fish, and a consensus is reached. As time passes and neither of you have connected with a fish – and you know you have the right flies on your cast, at the correct depth, because you determined this on a practice day before the competition – where, oh where, are the fish now? Then you both spot ten or so boats that have bunched together in a small area of the lake – they must be catching. You agree to motor over to that area, because boats attract other boats regardless of whether any are catching fish. I have been taught by better anglers than me that it is good to be skeptical, that you join the flotilla at the back so all the boats are in view, and count the number of fish caught in thirty minutes (whilst you fish, of course) so we have, say twenty anglers (two to a boat) catching eight fish, averaging sixteen fish over an hour, which is less than one per angler. If this is the case, it's time to move to another area – staying will not be productive enough to come in with a good bag.

As mentioned in Chapter 4, competition fishermen seem to love a class of fly called 'Blobs', and they catch a lot of fish with them. There is no delicacy in the tying – no thorax teased out with a dubbing needle to represent legs, no hint of an insect's tail tied with a few strands of feather, just, well, just a mass of bright sparkly cactus chenilles in sunburst, chartreuse, candy, coral and orange, tied onto a hook. Fishermen move them fast through the water, and stocky rainbows seem to love them, but it is a different matter when you fish for the wild brown trout of Scotland or Ireland, who ignore them completely. It seems that wild brown trout don't go a bundle on confections created by men. I have never fished with blobs, but that is a personal choice. You need to expend a great deal of energy in casting and then stripping back the flies at a furious pace, and I am unwilling to exert myself at the level required.

One reason I opted out of competitive fly fishing was that it ties you into fishing when there is little productive fishing to be had. I now go when the weather is kind, with cloud and a gentle breeze, but on many occasions, practice days feature howling winds and torrential downpours. You go out in wet-weather gear that is supposed to be waterproof, but driving rain will defeat it – only oilskins of the type trawlermen wear will keep the rain out. As we fishermen might be a bit self-conscious about our sartorial sense, we don't don these garments, which makes for a miserable, fruitless day. If you and your team are serious, however, practice days are de rigeur, so that (in theory at least) by the time the competition begins you have learned enough to give the team an edge. Once a member of our team, who couldn't make the day of the competition, was replaced by a well-known angling writer and photographer who stepped in at the last moment. On the competition day we supplied him with all the information we had learnt in practice. He came in with a below-average two trout at the end of the competition, and complained, "I thought you said the trout were in Spring Bay?" to which a team member replied, "they swim around, you know". Just one reason why practice days can be utterly pointless.

Rutland Water was, and still is, where most of the national finals were held, and where the best teams in the country ended up. The weather always seemed to be an issue on Rutland Water, a huge lake. A team member in one of my earliest forays into competition fishing suffered from seasickness and collapsed on the bottom of the boat, such were the waves that day. On some of the two-day finals, I glugged down Red Bull instead of tea to try to maintain the level of concentration required. Our team never managed to get our hands on silverware, but a notable achievement (on paper at least) was when we won a competition on Chew Valley Lake and, in the process, beat the Czech world team, who were practicing on Chew because that year it happened to be a venue for the world fly fishing championships. A hollow victory, perhaps, because for them it was just a practice day. They presented a china tankard to each of our team members which I still display.

You never know who your competition partner will be. I have fished with some superb fishermen, and even with a world fly fishing champion once on a tough day on Chew, where he caught just one more fish than me. Personal success evaded me. In three of the six years I was a competition angler I qualified to fish the English national final, where one hundred anglers compete for twenty places that make up the English team for the following year. I came close but didn't quite get there. I have no regrets – there was greater pleasure in just fishing, rather than competition fishing.

Whilst my friends continued with competition fishing, I was still able to 'pleasure fish' with them, both in the UK and abroad. This time we were in Montana: big sky country. We came to fish the Beaverhead River, one of the state's thousands of rivers and creeks. Western Montana has seventy-seven named mountain ranges, all part of the Rocky Mountains, and is bounded by three Canadian provinces and four of the United States. It is slightly larger than Japan and, after Alaska, California and Texas, is the largest state in America. It is even less densely populated than New Zealand, with one million people living in an area which is over 50% larger than the UK, though unsurprisingly so, as the rugged terrain of the Rocky Mountains doesn't lend itself to a large population. Many parts of the countryside are arid, and it seems at first that this is an unwelcoming, even unfriendly place. But the people, scarce as they are, and the wild beauty of this state, makes it unique and memorable – at least to me. I feel at home when I visit Montana.

The Beaverhead River begins at Clark Canyon dam and flows for 80 miles into the confluence of the Jefferson River. We had come to its banks for a 'float trip' that would take us 15 miles downstream. A float trip is when two anglers alight and take up positions in bow and stern of a rowing boat, in the middle of which sits an oarsman. His job is not to row, as the boat will career down the river's flow, but to back-row to slow the boat. When we come to an area which, in his considerable experience of the Beaverhead, holds fish, he endeavors to keep the boat stationary to allow the anglers to put in their flies.

The Beaverhead isn't a wide river and it twists and turns through the hills, its banks lined with willow and cottonwood trees. The three people in this boat are Andrew, the fishermen, Ed, the rower and guide, and myself. Sitting in the middle, Ed works the oars with his great muscled arms. He is young and fit and does this most days. I suspect when the fishing season is closed, he fells trees as a lumberjack, his arms certainly mighty enough to convincingly wield an axe. Unlike his Irish counterpart, Michael, whom we have known for several years and socialise with easily, Ed we don't know. He is one of several guides and we have never met him before the day of the float. There is no small talk; he is a taciturn fellow, and anyway, we want nothing but to fish. He tells us to cast slightly downstream towards the banks. We are using small Pheasant Tail and God Ribbed Hare's Ear nymphs, slightly weighted, so they sink just a little before we catch up with them in the boat and must recast. When casting towards the bank, sometimes a misjudgment in casting results in the fly hitting the bank. If it becomes snagged you have to tug it immediately and hope it comes away – if it doesn't, you lose the fly and have to retie another on your leader. A moving boat takes no prisoners, and no guide will bring the boat to the bank for you to disentangle the fly snagged in the undergrowth.

We stop for lunch, the boat hauled up a shingle beach. Andrew and I have had a great morning, hooking many trout, but landing maybe only half, which is fine with us – all would be returned anyway. Drinking wine and eating a packed lunch, for the first time I realise that mid-September temperatures in Montana aren't very warm. Reaching for my jacket, I notice on the gunnels a huge fly. What's that? I ask Ed. He puffs on the first cigarette he has had for some time and replies in a laconic way that I think all mid-western Americans use, "Caddis fly".

It is not that I am not familiar with caddis flies – called sedge flies in the UK – but these are huge compared with the ones that hatch on the lakes and reservoirs back home, and suddenly more and more are claiming the boat as a refuge: a hatch is taking place. "You might want to try this fly," says Ed, and hands me an Elk Hair Caddis fly pattern. I don't have any of these in my fly boxes, and gratefully accept his offer.

The Elk Hair Caddis fly was created in 1957 by Al Troth. Born in Pennsylvania in 1930, he began fishing at age twelve in local rivers and streams. Starting work at a Pittsburgh Steel factory, he left to join the navy and stayed there for four years. He then attended California State Teachers College, where he met his future wife, Martha Manandise. On graduation, he taught metalwork and woodwork in a machine shop at a local high school for fifteen years, fishing when he could, and became a skilful fly-tyer. Troth claimed that he didn't create the Elk Hair Caddis fly as a dry fly, now world-famous for being one, but that he wanted to develop a wet fly for use on his Pennsylvania streams. The pattern, with its spun elk-hair head and elk-hair wing, made it practically unsinkable, as elk hair is hollow and the air it retains makes the fly float like a cork. A talented, practical man, Troth was a writer of fishing articles, a photographer, a supreme fisherman and a fly tier, producing some beautiful flies, photos of which graced the cover of *Fly Fisherman Magazine* three times. Eventually, he couldn't resist the call of the Montana rivers that he fished in the summertime, and in 1973 he moved with his family to Dillon, a small town in the south-west of Montana, and started guiding on the Beaverhead and Big Hole Rivers.

Al Troth created many flies, but the Elk Hair Caddis is his most famous creation. Tom Rosenbauer, in his book *The Orvis guide to Essential American Flies*, devotes an entire chapter to it. Guiding for twenty-three years, he retired in 1996 with the onset of Parkinson's disease and dementia, and died in 2012. Sitting in that boat looking at this fly, I hadn't then known who Al Troth was, that he had created the fly I was now holding, or that I was fishing a river he loved to fish and guide other fishermen on. I think it was kismet.

Trout were now rising to this hatch of caddis flies about twenty yards upstream. As Andrew had disappeared behind some trees on a call of nature, I climbed out of the boat and waded carefully towards the rising fish. Behind me, Ed speaks: "They always seem to be rising there, but I haven't seen anyone that has managed to hook one".

I wade to the far bank, immediately below the rising fish, so I can get as natural a drift of my fly as I can, hoping it will be drag-free and that Al Troth's fly will work for me. Several casts later, nothing. The fly is being ignored. Andrew has returned to the boat, and I sense that he wants to continue with the float trip – we have several more miles to go. "A few more casts," I shout, about to conclude "and then we'll go," but before I could utter those words a brown trout, a good one, jumps out of the river. Though I don't see it take my fly, it is definitely on my line, hooked and unhappy with this interruption of its feeding on the hatching sedges. In a narrow river like the Beaverhead, with little real water depth, there aren't many places a fish can go, and keeping it on a reasonably tight line, I net the fish quickly.

Of the many fish I have caught, I have never witnessed such a perfect specimen. It wasn't big by Beaverhead standards, between 3-4lb, but the shape, colour, size and markings were perfect, the tail wide and with no trace of any blemishes, the head a proportionate size relative to its torpedo-shaped body. It was a supreme being created by nature. There is usually some little flaw or imperfection when I look at a fish, but not this one, this one had none. I don't have a photograph of it, as I didn't have a camera, and wouldn't go back to the boat to get one because I didn't want the fish to endure any further stress. I felt obligated to return it as quickly as I could.

Yellowstone National Park spills over the Montana border from Wyoming and Idaho. We were in southwestern Montana on an American trip that had already included fishing some rivers in Yellowstone. Eastern Montana is a land of prairies and a topography named 'Badlands'. The prairies were once home to the indigenous people known as the Plains Indians, who fought the US Calvary in the great Sioux war of 1876 after being robbed of their land. At the Battle of Little Bighorn in 1876 all 210 men under General Custer's command were killed by a large force of Lakota, Cheyenne and Arapaho Native Americans. Historians consider 'Custer's last stand' and its battle plan controversial, and President Ulysses S. Grant, himself a successful general in the American Civil War, believed Custer unnecessarily caused his own death and the death of his men. Little Bighorn sadly hastened the demise of the Plains Indians, as they were ultimately corralled into reservations, their land confiscated. The Sioux, threatened with the withholding of rations to their reservation, agreed to cede the Black Hills of Dakota, but never accepted the legitimacy of the forced deprivation of their Black Hills reservation and finally, after many legal battles, in 1980 the Supreme Court ruled on the side of the Sioux. Compensation was awarded for one billion US dollars, however the Sioux declined, because acceptance would legally terminate Sioux demands for the return of the Black Hills.

The money remains in a 'Bureau of Indian Affairs Account', accruing compound interest.

America's long and tortured relationship with issues of race, subjugation, and white supremacy, both past and present, is surely beyond the limited scope of this book, and my own experiences as a white man. However, in travelling the world, encountering the varied cultures of places like New Zealand, America, even closer to home in Wales, I find myself obligated to acknowledge how completely different life experiences are for white people in contrast with populations of colour. It brings to mind a work of fiction *Human Stain*, by Philip Roth, a master of American literature, in which a boy is born white in a black family, and, as he grows older, recognises the undeniable reality of structural racism and how it plays out in the lives of black people.

It occurred to me as I read this book that a large factor in racism is tribal, and I have written already about our propensity for belonging to a group. For instance, a person born in Cornwall would consider himself Cornish, then English, then British and then there are so many sub-sections after that such as politics, sport, religion etc. But none of those things can be so universally experienced and ingrained in human experience as the question of skin colour. Perhaps this is due to the physical visibility of skin colour, as much as anything else – I could tell you how many black anglers I have met in my fishing career, but would not be confident in saying how many anglers were Cornish, or socialists, or Jewish, or Arsenal supporters. In Bill Bryson's marvellous book *The Body*, in his chapter on the skin, he recounts how a professor incised and peeled back a sliver of skin about a millimetre thick from the arm of a cadaver. It was so thin as to be translucent. "'That,' he said, 'is where all your skin colour is. That's all that race is - a sliver of epidermis.'" Bryson mentions this to Professor Nina Jablonski, Professor of Anthropology at Penn State University, who says it is extraordinary how such a small facet of our composition is given so much importance. People act as if skin colour is a determinant of character when all it is is a reaction to sunlight. Biologically, there is actually no such thing as race – nothing in terms of skin colour, facial features: hair type, bone structure or anything else that is a defining quality amongst peoples. And yet look how many people have been enslaved, or hated, or lynched, or deprived of fundamental rights through history because of the colour of their skin.

In fact, over many years of fly fishing, I have never encountered a black angler, and even as I look at the riverbanks of my memory at the course fishermen angling for roach, pike, and perch, I cannot recall ever meeting one. Black anglers must exist, but in my experience, they are a rarity and it's strange that this is so. If I then recall any day-to-day contact with a black person, it is astonishing that I have had none since I was fifteen, when I was working at a wool warehouse where a typist named Kay, from Jamaica, was also employed. How has this extraordinary situation of no-contact occurred? People of colour have historically been kept together and separate from the white population by societal pressures and a subtle, and often not-so-subtle, racism. Institutionalised discrimination and marginalisation lead to fewer and more limiting job opportunities, less suitable housing, and a documented imbalance in the quality of healthcare, which in many cases has an impact on health and life expectancy, and people of colour are subject to illness to a degree not experienced by white people. A remarkable programme on BBC4, *Extra Life: A Short History of Living Longer*, presented by Steven Johnson and David Olusoga, recently featured an analysis of why Covid 19 was more deadly in Black and Asian populations, and an interview with the head of The Human Genome Project was asked what DNA differences there was between white, black and Asian people. He answered 'none'. White, black, and Asian people share 99.99% of the same DNA, so your race doesn't make you more or less susceptible to a deadly outcome. What caused Covid 19 to be more deadly to someone who wasn't white? In his opinion, and also that of the two presenters, inherent racism has caused comorbidities like high blood pressure, stress and other serious maladies that affects general health, that has made black and Asian populations more vulnerable. Racism, it seems, also kills.

I have recently finished a book that I would never have normally read, by an author I hadn't heard of before. It wouldn't have even brushed the edge of my consciousness, and I certainly wouldn't have downloaded it onto my Kindle, had a paperback copy my daughter left on a table not caught my eye with its intriguing title, *Why I'm No Longer Talking To White People About Race*. It proves the value of the printed word, and physical copies of books that others can read – my downloads are only accessible by myself and would catch no-one's eye.

Reni Eddo-Lodge published a post on her blog with this title in 2014 and, three years later, published her first book with the same name. She then became the first black British author to top the UK bestseller lists. Eddo-Lodge was born in 1989 and raised in London by her Nigerian mother. She attended the University of Central Lancashire, studied English and graduated in 2011. She is now an award-winning journalist writing for, amongst other publications, the *New York Times*, the *Daily Telegraph*, the *Guardian* and the *Independent*. Her book has won many plaudits, been named 2018 Book of the Year a Writer of Colour, and gained several literary awards. So what possible insight can I, a white man, bring to a book written by a black woman about race? If I agree with everything she has written, why don't I just entreat others to go and buy the book and read it? I feel that there is a kind of presumptuousness to commenting on her writing and her exploration of the dichotomy that exists between black and white people, that she has done both forcefully and elegantly. I am going to give it a go, though, because it is one of the most important books I have read, and it has changed the way I perceive race for good.

There are many reasons why this is an uncomfortable book to read if you are white. I found myself wincing at truths I had never been aware of, such as discussions of structural racism and white privilege that almost always negatively impact the lives of black people. In our predominantly white society, I, being white, have an advantage that I may not personally be aware of, but which has inevitably had an impact on the course of my life. Feeling as I do that I have worked hard, struggled, achieved, and failed on my own terms, and with only myself to thank and to blame, having suddenly to acknowledge the influence of an undeniable and essentially evil power structure is a confronting and unwelcome thought. But does being white make me a racist? Does benefiting from something I had until now been unaware of make me complicit? Is the fact that I had been unaware of something so impactful on society make me racist? I had never questioned myself before about this, but I am part of white society that practices, by default, structural racism, and benefits from what Eddo-Lodge calls "white privilege" and "the system". Eddo-Lodge explains best:

> To some, the word privilege in the context of whiteness invokes images of a life lived in the lap of luxury, enjoying the spoils of the super-rich. When I talk about white privilege, I don't mean that white people have it easy, that they've never struggled, or that they've never lived in poverty. But white privilege is the fact that if you're white, your race will almost certainly positively impact your life's trajectory in some way and you probably won't even notice it. [...] White privilege is dull, grinding complacency. It is par for the course in a world in which drastic race inequality is responded to with a shoulder shrug, considered just the norm.

Well-meaning white people adopt a strategy of colour blindness to help mitigate the subconscious negativity that we might face when we really think about race. In his book, *Freedom from the Known*, one of Kristnamurti's themes is a world where prejudice and bias become unavailable, and though it might be regarded as utopian it is nevertheless unobtainable. Eddo-Lodge writes that:

> Structural racism is never a case of innocent and pure, persecuted people of colour versus white people intent on evil and malice. Rather, it is about how Britain's

relationship with race infects and distorts equal opportunity. Structural racism is dozens, or hundreds, or thousands of people with the same biases joining together to make up one organisation and acting accordingly. Structural racism is an impenetrably white workplace culture set by those people, where anyone who falls outside of the culture must conform or face failure.

It is tempting to continue to quote Eddo-Lodge at length, like any book that has had a real and profound impact, I want to tell everyone as much as I can about what she has to say, and I cannot hope to match her eloquence or her insight if I were to try to paraphrase. I will limit myself to one last selection, and at the same time implore you to purchase your own copy, find it in a library or download it, as it is worth all the discomfort you might experience:

> When we live in the age of colour-blindness and fool ourselves with the lie of meritocracy, some will have to be silent in order for others to thrive. [...] Repeatedly telling ourselves – and worse still, telling our children – that we are all equal is a misdirected yet well-intentioned lie. Indulging in the myth that we are all equal denies the economic, political and social legacy of a British society that has historically been organised by race. The reality is that, in material terms, people of colour are nowhere near equal.

Today this book has irreversibly altered my perception on race, but what can I consider the positive impact it has had on me to be? I have posed the question of whether by being white and benefiting from white culture, white history, I am therefore tainted with a racism that I cannot avoid. I thought I surely couldn't be racist, but now I'm not so sure, even if the dictionary definition in its noun and adjective forms aren't, I think, really applicable to me. When I meet people of colour, I have come to realise that the life of that person may have included long bouts of disadvantages, continual frustrations and thwarted ambitions because of the colour of their skin.

The next day we moved on to Wyoming. Our journey, some 200 miles to Jackson Hole, took a little over three hours. The float trip down the Beaverhead had proved to be so successful that we tipped Ed a further 50 dollars and purred our appreciation for his skills in constantly putting us on fish. Jackson Hole is a valley some 48 miles long and Jackson, where we would be staying, and the gateway to Yellowstone and Grand Teton National parks, was a picturesque town of two-storey buildings that owed its architecture to mid-nineteenth century small-town America, the sort of place Norman Rockwell made famous in his paintings. It's a step back in time; no skyscrapers. Real estate here is some of the most expensive in America, and it is an outdoorsy type of place, with skiing and snowboarding hugely popular on its slopes in the winter. Jackson Hole hosts an annual symposium by the Federal Reserve Bank of Kansas, where central bankers and financial organisations from 70 countries come to discuss matters of a financial nature.

Within the valley of Jackson Hole, two miles from Jackson, is the watercourse we had come to fish, Flat Creek. Winding its way through the National Elk Refuge, established in 1912 to preserve the Jackson elk herd, and which has become the largest wintering concentration of elk in the world, Flat Creek, well, earns its name. It is in a valley which is surrounded by mountains, and there are no trees and few bushes. It is very flat, mainly sage grass, but is a prolific cutthroat trout water, though only open for three months of the year, from August to October. Like the New Zealand rivers I had fished, it requires a stealthiness of approach because there is no cover. Just walking up to its water would scatter any fish in the vicinity.

"Walk a while before you start fishing," a local had said, sipping the Jack Daniels we bought him to loosen his tongue. No fisherman worth his salt would give out specific information about their fishery, so we were only after general information. "The first couple of miles gets heavily fished, get away from that and you have a chance of picking up a fish or two," he concluded. So we did that, walking past quite a few fishermen – Andrew yomping ahead of me – hoping to reach uncrowded and productive water. With or without cover to hide you, stealth is essential to ensnaring a wild trout. On this tough water, we adopted a strategy learned in New Zealand: wear dull clothing, because bright clothing alerts fish and makes them scurry to the undercut banks; they will spot you long before you have a chance to see them. We could cast our flies only when we saw a fish rise, and we wouldn't see them rise without stalking them, keeping low to hide against the flat horizon. We targeted the many bends of the river where fish lie in wait, as the water bounces off the curve of the bank, bringing with it much of the fishes' larder.

We did well and caught some lovely looking cutthroat trout, myself using a small black Elk Hair Caddis fly, Andrew using a small Hopper fly, which imitated some of the terrestrials being blown onto the water's surface. Lessons learnt in New Zealand, and the local's advice to 'go far,' had made it a memorable day.

| 10 |

Lough Corrib in a Caenis hatch

Caenis

There are plenty of places in the world I haven't yet fished: for sea trout on the Rio Grande in Argentina, for salmon on the Kola Peninsula in Russia, for steelhead in British Columbia – but with the physical encumbrances age brings about, I find myself fishing much closer to home these days — such as on Lough Corrib, on a fine June morning. It was 5am, and the sun, rising rapidly, bathed the lake in a bright golden glow. Despite the tiredness I felt, having risen an hour earlier, I realised that there were few places in the world that I would rather be.

Lough Corrib is a huge lake in the West of Ireland, with a surface area of 68 square miles, bordered to the South and East by attractive vistas of pastoral land, and to the West and North by bogs that have now acquired ecological importance in the fight against climate change. William Wilde, father of Oscar, wrote a book about Lough Corrib and its islands, and built a summerhouse on its shore. The lake has an outlet to the Atlantic Ocean at Galway City via the Corrib River. We had come to Lough Corrib, my fishing buddy and I, to fish for wild brown trout, catching them on a small dry fly that imitated a caenis, the smallest fly in the mayfly family.

To my knowledge no-one has created a specific 'pattern' for caenis, as few actively fish for trout using a dry fly imitation. It is, I suppose, the most generic version of a fly in my fly box, with just a few wisps of feather tied onto a small white body as a tail and wing. Caenis hatch in their thousands, and it is so difficult to catch trout that feed on them that they are known as 'the angler's curse'. The trout seem to take on the characteristics of basking sharks and just swim around with their mouths open, without targeting any individual caenis. This is bad news for anyone who wants the fish to take their individual fly.

Whilst most fishermen would pack up fishing when caenis are about, we were actively seeking them out, trying to catch the fish that fed on them, using tiny flies to represent the plentiful mayfly. My fishing buddy, and partner on this trip, had learnt from his Irish contacts that prolific hatches of caenis were taking place. This could be a now or never opportunity to try our luck – and luck would be what we needed, lots of it. Why were we trying to do something that other anglers regarded as madness? Were we just plain delusional, or had some sort of vanity taken hold? Heaven only knows why we had come to catch trout – and I would be happy to catch just one – using a tiny fly, fished dry, amongst multitudes. I suppose if we were mountaineers, having a crack at Mount Everest would be the pinnacle of our ambition. In that case preparation would be key to our success, if we had the skillset.

That day on the lake we could prepare till the cows come home, but skillset or not, luck was what we really needed to connect with any trout in the midst of a caenis hatch.

When we entered Ballindiff Bay, we cut the noisy engine. Ballindiff was home to some recent extraordinary hatches of caenis, or so the locals told us when we plied them with Guinness and Bushmill whiskey the night before. We would use oars from now on. We were two anglers on bow and stern, but only one of us would fish at a time, to minimise our presence on the water. We could easily spook these fast-moving, surface-feeding trout if we both fished at the same time. I would go first, and there was a solitary dry Caenis fly on my leader. I could tie these tiny flies, but they were fiddlesome, so I bought them from a professional fly-tyer. The tippet (nylon) had to be thin to thread it through the eye of the hook, small as it was, with 3lb breaking strain nylon – 4lb being the maximum that would fit through the eye.

The mayflies were gone, apart from a few stragglers, and the lake olives too. The duckfly (known to us as 'buzzers') had also vanished, not to return until early spring next year. We had anxiously scanned the weather a week prior to our trip, because caenis hatch only in certain conditions, mainly in the early morning or at dusk, and prefer water with little or no ripple, with a gentle, warm breeze. They are very, very fussy about when to pop their heads out of the water, and I suppose because these conditions occur rarely on this huge lough, when they do, massive hatches occur. The outlook seemed bleak as we scanned the water for signs of a caenis hatch. We waited. The sun climbed higher into the sky, and still we waited. Glancing to my right, I noticed birds swooping down onto the water. "Matt, over there!" I shouted. He trained his binoculars on the area.

"Yes, there are swallows feeding – picking up food from the surface – Caenis?"

"Let's have a look," I said, grateful that these marvellous little visitors from Africa had shown us the way. I worked the oars quietly, then not one, but three areas, each about 100 square meters, erupted with the little white fly that was also beginning to cover the boat gunwales, and trout were there – so many trout – feasting on them by slurping their way through the densely populated caenis. I made ready with my rod, pulling the flyline from the reel, high on adrenaline but low on anticipation – for this was surely madness – and cast to the closest pocket of caenis and fish some fifteen meters away. Although my cast was good, my tiny fly was just one amongst many thousands of natural caenis. After a fruitless hour I made way for Matthew. The hatch wouldn't go on for much longer, and could end at any time, so he had to have a crack at them whilst it was still happening. Then, as the caenis subsided, with fewer flies on the water, Matt hooked and landed a brown trout, a typically beautifully proportioned Corrib fish, around 2lb. I guess that the simple fact that there were now fewer flies meant that fish were targeting the individuals that were left, and he got lucky. But I don't really believe in a 'lucky' Matt, for he is an exceptional angler. Fishing his local well-stocked put-and-take fishery back home, where you are charged per pound of fish you caught, he would snip off the business end of the hook, including the barb, so fish might 'take' the fly but swim away again unharmed. The pleasure was just in fooling the fish and not hooking them.

When we fish, we knowingly enter an alien realm – water – and we are fascinated with its creatures, which are part of our world but not of it. We pit our brains, and our knowledge, against their instincts, honed over millions of years. So we fish with bait or fly for them, and if you want to eat them, that is okay, but if you want to kill and photograph them for no more than an egocentric purpose, that is not. If we have had our sport in capturing the fish, or just in the electricity that surged through our bodies when we felt it on our line, then fishing has served its purpose, for me, at least.

We headed back to our hotel for a late breakfast, a rest, then went back to the water – this time using other fly patterns. We caught two browns that took a Mayfly nymph, then returned to our hotel in the late afternoon, and a meal before bed at 8pm, to rise again at 4am for our last morning's tilt at our crazy dream of catching fish in a caenis hatch. We had come for just two days fishing; longer than that would require greater motivation than either of us had. Two days in which to catch or not, two days and that's it – continuing into any more days would just delay our failure and weaken our resolve, and if we caught in two days, then home it was, mission accomplished.

In 2010 Kathryn Schulz wrote a book, *Being Wrong: Adventures in the Margin of Error*, that has only grown in relevance. The book is about being wrong, and within it she coins the phrase 'wrongology', which she describes as the science of seeing potential upsides in your errors, and fighting the perception that error is always bad. Why is it more prescient ten years after it was published? Today we have the worst, most polarised and toxic attitudes since the 1930s, where conspiracy theories flourish and the role of satire, the use of humour, exaggeration, or ridicule to expose and criticise stupidity or vice, is now redundant: there are so many versions of truth now, depending on what is acceptable to you, your worldview and personal experiences, that satire no longer serves a purpose as satire – it has melded into another 'truth'.

This crazy, mixed-up world is in large part due to insidious social media platforms that, along with the likes of Cambridge Analytica and interventions from foreign hackers, helped to persuade some seventy million voters to back a man that has been proven – in his four years of office – to be little short of a despot, and destroyed the myth that democracy is a 'given' that will always be sacrosanct. In the two-hour documentary *The Great Hack* by directors Karim Amer and Jehane Noujaim, we see how the symbiotic relationship between social media platforms and Cambridge Analytica allowed so many to be manipulated into holding polarised and toxic views and to see them as indisputable 'truth'. This documentary is a must-see. At the time of the storming of the Capitol in Washington, I recall a CNN News commentator saying that as long as social media outlets foment so many conspiracy theories, there will be no civil society. Shortly afterwards, Facebook and Twitter banned Donald Trump from using their platforms and Apple, Google and Amazon withdrew the applications necessary to access right-wing media platform, Parler.

In this modern dichotomy we must hope that, on quiet reflection, enough of us can realise when we might have been misguided, misinformed, or just wrong. There's the rub: this is a hugely difficult thing to do, but by not admitting where you have been mistaken, you continue to pursue a path that is against both your interests and those of society in general, such as voting for a crook, or accepting a statement that was touted on the side of a bus in the Brexit debate.

I have to confess that I am no angel, and have argued for a position that I really didn't know was either right or wrong at the time. In the first fly fishing club I joined I became a 'fixer', arranging for well-known and prominent fly fishermen to attend our club to give us talks. When I invited a quite famous individual (at least to us) I invited members of another local club to attend – a much bigger club than ours who had a highly respected club chairman. I engaged him in a conversation about what was the most skilful method of fly fishing: from bank or boat? I had changed my method to fishing from a boat, and argued vehemently that of course, boat fishing required more skill, but he was a bank fisherman and was of a different opinion. I argued passionately that I was right, but there was no rationale to prove or disprove my theory. I had fallen into the trap of believing something because I wanted to believe it. I now know this is a moot point; fishing from bank and boat probably aren't comparable in a way that means one is 'better' than the other, rather that they are different in certain ways that make them suited to some and not others, depending on your preferences. It doesn't matter what discipline is best, you just fish the way you want to.

Schulz can rescue us from these misadventures in our thinking, because 'wrongology', as she explains it, means that humans are humans because very often they get it wrong and, indeed, being wrong can promote individual growth. Kathryn Schulz, born in Shaker Heights, Ohio, is the daughter of Margot Schulz, a teacher, and Isaac Schulz, a lawyer. She graduated from Brown University in 1996 and became a freelance writer published in the *New York Times*, *Rolling Stone* and the *Nation*. She began her career as a journalist and editor on environmental, labour and human rights issues for the *Santiago Times* in Chile, and was for a time editor for the online environmental magazine *Grist*. In 2015 she became a staff reporter for the *New Yorker* and in 2016 she won a Pulitzer Prize for feature writing. This book, her only one, garnered plaudits galore from some august publications: the *New Scientist* called it "a compelling meditation on the human condition...Schulz exposes the psychological tricks we play on ourselves when we cling to beliefs in the face of evidence."

At the beginning, she extrapolates on why we regard ourselves as right:

> A whole lot of us go through life assuming that we are basically right, basically all of the time, about basically everything: about our political and intellectual convictions, our religious and moral beliefs, our assessment of other people, our memories, our grasp of facts. As absurd as it sounds when we stop to think about it, our steady state seems to be one of unconsciously assuming that we are very close to omniscient.

How right she is about how wrong we can be. How we can muddle through believing that our upbringing, our beliefs, mustn't be questioned: of course, we are the righteous ones! Being human, to paraphrase Schulz, we can't help feeling jubilant when we acknowledge other people's mistakes: "not only was I right, I was also right about being right. In the instance of uttering it, I become right squared, maybe, even right factorial. Logarithmically right – at any rate, really extremely right and really, extremely delighted about it". She has described me perfectly; I readily admit to experiencing this. I just like to be right – I can't help it – but knowing this about myself and acknowledging it, I can try to reach an understanding with this 'righteousness' that I insist upon. I can also look more kindly on the people who, after four years of serious misdemeanours and outright crimes by Donald Trump, still voted for him in their millions. Why – conspiracy theories and uncensored falsehoods spread by social media didn't help, but what about the people themselves, who are they? It is possible to view another person's Facebook page to a greater or lesser extent, and though you may argue my investigation was not morally rigorous, after viewing maybe a dozen of pages of people posting about the fraudulent election and other right-wing topics, all I could find aside from these posts, were ordinary people with very much the same comments about family, pets and general life experiences as would appear on any page. As humans we can't help having opinions – beliefs that are born from our life experiences and influenced by our class, our colour, our heredity – and we can't dodge them, we are at one with them. If not fully embedded into our psyche, a belief can sometimes be acknowledged as wrong without grave existential consequences, to be replaced by another belief. As Schulz writes, "we are absolutely right about something up until the very instant that, lo and behold, we are absolutely right about something else". It is the big beliefs that we must reconcile within ourselves should they be proved wrong, "beliefs so important and far-reaching that we can neither easily replace them nor easily live without them – these gigantic beliefs collapse like stars, leaving only us and a black hole behind."

Schulz's writing becomes more serious and consequential when she reviews what happens when a major copper-bottomed belief turns into a rusty old tin, namely the realisation that you have not only got some-thing wrong, but that the wrongness is gut-wrenching and visceral. These beliefs of a big religious, political, or personal nature, that have betrayed the principles dear to you, result in this phenomenon of pure wrongness. She concludes "The thing about fully experiencing wrong-ness is it strips us of all our theories, including theories about ourselves. This isn't fun while it's happening – it leaves us feeling flayed, laid bare to the bone and the world – but it does make possible that rarest of occurrences: real change."

To paraphrase Schulz as rightly as I can, we (wrongly) interpret other people's views due to three assumptions: the ignorance assumption, the idiocy assumption and the evil assumption. The first, the ignorance assumption, is, she says "since we think our own beliefs are based on facts, we conclude that people who disagree with us just haven't been exposed to the right information and that such exposure would invariably bring them over to our team." She cites both religious evangelism and political activism as examples of assuming that it is possible to change what people believe by educating them. She points out that this is not always wrong for the reasons that we think: "the facts might be sufficiently ambiguous to support multiple interpretations. When other people reject our beliefs, we think they lack good information. When we reject their beliefs, we think we possess good judgment." Concerning the idiocy assumption, we believe that our opponents have the facts, but are too stupid to comprehend them. This assessment applies not only to individuals, but to any group that is regarded as the opposition. In the evil assumption, we simply think that people who earn this mantle know the truth and comprehend it, but wilfully turn their backs on it.

In all these views we are striving for certainty, but there is really no such thing – even in science, every truth is only a truth until it is disproved through research and study, and the theories of a hundred years or so are today mostly invalidated because they are all there to be tested, built upon and developed into other, perhaps temporary, truths. So we might ask ourselves if there is any point in searching for an ultimate truth which can never reveal itself? The need for certainty in us is powerful, and it helps in selecting our leaders. In the 2004 presidential election, which gave G.W. Bush the presidency over John Kerry, the inevitable post-mortems conducted as to why Kerry came to lose to Bush – given that Bush's first term was less than inspirational – concluded that Kerry put off many voters because they thought he changed his mind on a few important issues, whilst Bush never wavered from his convictions. There is a quote by John Maynard Keynes, "when the facts change, I change my mind." But voters didn't take that view because, well, the high-flyers who lead us aren't supposed to conduct U-turns. The present British Prime Minister, Boris Johnson, is often lambasted by the press for his frequent U-turns, mainly relating to his Covid policies. I didn't vote for him, and regard him as one of the worst Prime Ministers in recent history, but Schulz comments that "we like our leaders to be super-confident even if they are wrong because we are more alarmed by leaders who waver than by those who screw up." Our man in Number 10 seems capable of doing both! Schulz writes that the 2004 U.S. election was "truly one of history's finest examples of a contest between a man who wavered and a man who screwed up."

I am the least practical person my wife knows, which didn't bode well for becoming a competent fisherman. I came to it late, bringing nothing to the table, while others, who enjoyed the sport as boys, fishing with a worm or maggot, unencumbered by theories or expectations, drew on their experiences and seemed to be naturals whatever the discipline. I wasn't very good in my early days – not a natural fisherman. If I saw a fish had risen, I would cast my fly there. Others explained that doing that meant you were too late – the fish had moved on. By watching the signs that feeding fish exhibited on the surface water, direction and speed could be ascertained, and a fly cast with enough 'forward lead' in the right direction. This can produce results but, of course, you still need a fly on your cast that the trout want to eat! For all that I have written about dry-fly fishing, it is the sunk flies – the underwater nymphs and larvae of the fly that hatch on the surface – that I have fished the most of. Here, the fly is unseen, somewhere in the water at an unknown depth, and success can depend on trying to visualise a 3D map inside your head, showing just where the fish might be in the water. If you have three flies on your cast, they will all be at different depths, for a fly nearest a floating fly line will be highest in the water, held up by the buoyant fly line, and won't sink so much as the fly that is tied to the end of the cast, which will be deepest in the water. Visualisation is the nearest word I can find to describe it, as it's more a feeling, a kind of premonition, really. Some days you are better at it than others, and it all adds to the magic of this sport for me.

Paying attention to the probabilities of where you feel the fish are likely to be, together with the visible behaviour of the fish, is the difference between a successful angler and those who fail to catch.

My fishing life has had its fair number of downs as well as ups, though I wouldn't change any of the experiences I have had. The famous quote by golfer Gary Player, "the more I practice the luckier I get," is certainly appropriate to fishing, but it is the process of improvement rather than the success you might have, the journey that takes you from beginner to old hand, no matter the final skill level, that I think is the best part of fishing. Problem-solving abilities and a practical mindset might make for a better fisherman – but I can now compete simply through years of accumulated experience. I caught one fish in the morning, the day we left Lough Corrib, and managed to land it – a bit of a feat when the hook is so small that the gap, the business end containing the barb, is tiny, and the hook-hold minimal. Holding my breath, I steered the fish to the net with as little force as I could, and relief washed over me. Alleluia! Success on the Corrib!

| 11 |

Red Kites over Clywedog Reservoir

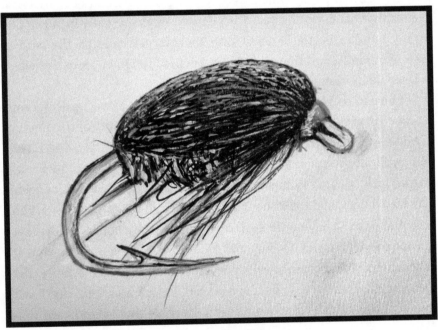

Coch Y Bonddu

Clywedog Reservoir, set in the beautiful countryside of mid-Wales, is one of the most picturesque waters I have fished. Its beauty is often overshadowed by the more well-known areas of Snowdonia and the Brecon Beacons that are not far away. Having lived in a city for most of my life, now that I have moved to Wales I am a committed countryphile, so pleased to live amongst its hills, mountains, valleys, rivers, streams and forests. It's different from anywhere else I have lived – Germany where I was born, Cambridgeshire, Lincolnshire, and Somerset, where I grew up with my family in RAF married quarters – but for the greatest part of my life, in the city of Bristol. There are many good reasons for living in such places, but they don't trump what this beautiful countryside can offer, full of a diversity of birds, animals and landscapes. And, of course, sheep are everywhere, in every field, however small: sometimes it looks like they are in people's gardens! In Wales, there are more sheep than people.

Andrew and I had come to Clywedog to fish over two days for rainbow and brown trout, which were feasting on a bonanza of territorial beetles that hatch once a year for just two weeks, usually in June. The coch y bondhu beetle hatches from their larval stage on the land in their thousands, and the adult flying beetles are blown onto the water in large quantities.

The road to Hafren Forest also accesses the Clywedog Reservoir, reached from the north by the B4518, some miles short of the town of Llanidloes. The turning marked 'Hafren Forest and Clywedog Reservoir' will take you along the scenic perimeter of the lake. The road, a single track, meanders through fields of wandering sheep, unencumbered by fences, and the grass is a vivid emerald green with a sparkling brightness that I have only ever seen before in Ireland. A bridge over one of the tributaries feeding the reservoir leads you to the forest's edge, then into a series of hills and dips. A stretch of the forest here seems scarred, as harvested trees have left a barrenness that sits ill with the fecundity of the surrounding land. Leaving this behind, two miles further is the turnoff to Clywedog Reservoir. The car clatters down a steep road, across the ubiquitous railings that corral the sheep and thwart their bids for freedom. I can glimpse on my left the narrow beginnings of one of the reservoir's arms. The lake now begins to display its stunning scenery. It is possible to look at it too much whilst driving, as you may end up in the water if you don't keep the required concentration.

The forest was created in 1937, covering 15 square miles, for the planting and felling of pine and spruce trees for newspaper, chipboard, fencing and wood for the construction industry. The source of the River Severn is high up on the slopes of Pumlumon, the highest mountain in mid-Wales, one mile from its border. Buzzards, goshawks, red kites, merlin and sparrowhawks, crossbills and nightjars all find a home there, as well as, recently, ospreys from Africa, who visit for the summer. Walking trails through the forest are well used by tourists and locals. Clywedog Reservoir itself was completed in 1967 after a four-year construction programme and was created by damming the Afon (River) Clywedog, a tributary of the Severn. It covers 615 acres, and although not a wide reservoir – only 500 meters at its widest point – it is very long, with several arms jutting out from its main body. In 1966 a bomb was detonated within the construction site, and it was suspected that a para-military group connected to Welsh nationalism was responsible. Welsh nationalists knew that Clywedog was being built as a supply reservoir for the city of Birmingham, just as previous reservoirs had been built for the city of Liverpool, and it rankled that these lands had been flooded for English benefit. They had a point: the English gave the Celtic nations of this United Kingdom a raw deal. Although there have been no highland clearances in Wales, no potato famine decimating the population, Wales has suffered many injustices at the hands of English barons, lords and kings.

Conflict looms large throughout the history of Wales, initially between Welsh kingdoms as they fought for overall supremacy. After the Norman conquest they came under the sway of the English crown, before wrangling back the greater part of control by 1101. What followed was a cycle of civil instability and repeated revolts against their increasingly aggressive English neighbours. Between 1277 and 1283, Edward I of England finally defeated and annexed the principality of Wales, building a ring of stone castles in strategic places to retain his conquered lands – though they couldn't halt occasional attacks against the occupiers. Just a few miles from my home is the site of the Welsh parliament of Owain Glyndwr, the last Welshman to hold the title of Prince of Wales. In September 1400, Owain Glyndwr instigated the Welsh revolt against Henry IV, and a brief golden age of Welsh independence followed. After successes in North and Central Wales, English forces ultimately prevailed, but today Owain Glyndwr retains a mythical status as a father of Welsh nationalism. The old Welsh parliament building at Machynlleth is a visitor attraction and café now, but I can feel when I go there the history that permeates this old building and seeps into the atmosphere of the place.

In 1536 Henry VIII banned the use of the Welsh language, stripping it of any official role. Although William Morgan gave it a significant boost when he translated the Bible into Welsh in 1588, the fight to retain Welsh was not won until 1993, when the Welsh Language Act established that the Welsh and English languages should be treated equally in the conduct of public business in Wales. It also gave Welsh Ministers the power to assign a Welsh name to any body, office or place to which legislation gives a title. In 2011, the Welsh Language (Wales) Measure gave the Welsh language equal status with that of English, and established bodies to protect and promote it, investigating any interference with the freedom to use Welsh. It was hard-won. In Welsh schools in the eighteenth, nineteenth and twentieth centuries, an item was used called the Welsh Not (not knot, but 'not') which took the form of a piece of wood, a ruler, or a stick, given to the first pupil heard speaking Welsh. When another child was heard using Welsh, the Not was given to the latest offender. Whoever was in possession of the Not was encouraged to pass it on to any of their Welsh-speaking classmates by informing the teacher that they had caught that person speaking Welsh. The pupil in possession of the Welsh Not at the end of the day was subjected to corporal punishment. It was a wicked system to encourage pupils not to speak their own language.

That first day on Clywedog, Welsh voices were loud on the boat jetty. Judging from their banter, their day had been successful. We mumbled that we had caught a few. A 'few' if said in the right tone can convey that really, we have caught more, but we are not the boastful sort and are too modest to detail exactly how many. Beware the successful angler who has had a good day, for they always, it seems, want to nail down exactly how many you have caught and will ask outright. Such a question requires an answer cloaked in obfuscation: "we had two to the boat" – so neither I nor my partner claimed to have caught the fish. The 'boat' saves a fellow angler from ignominy had he blanked and not caught anything. Two to the boat is the honourable answer – there is no other way. Pride is everything.

The subjugation of Wales only created a greater sense of identity amongst the Welsh peoples. The Welsh language, despite all efforts to eliminate it, did not die, and is still used in mid- and North Wales, though not so much in the South and West. Yearly Eisteddfods (festivals) enhance this sense of Welshness, and the Senedd, the Welsh Parliament, encourages and fights for all things Welsh. In contrast, England displays little of its identity. Perhaps this is because it is easier to be proud of the stalwart oppressed than of the oppressors – and perhaps it is easier to see ourselves in the world of sport, where our victories have not been so overwhelming, nor so bathed in others' disadvantages. Success or failure, therefore, has little correlation to a strong sense of pride on one's identity. Struggle is the admirable element – to struggle and fail, or to struggle and succeed – both can be worthy of pride, whether for a fisherman or a nation. But to take what you want at every step, suppress those that struggle, put down any who fail, and to expect success and plaudits at the cost of others; that is nothing to be proud of. Indeed, even privately, where is the pleasure in winning unopposed?

There is a story about a fly fisherman who, not living an entirely blameless life, passes away and finds himself on a beautiful chalk stream, with fish rising all around him. Fly rod in hand, he lays his fly on the water and a stunning two-and-a-half-pound rainbow trout takes his dry fly, which he lands. I must have gone to heaven, he concludes. The next cast produces the same result – yes, this must indeed be heaven. The next cast and the next cast after that yields the same and it suddenly begins to pall. He shouts, "Oh, hell," and the Riverkeeper, standing close by, says, "Correct". He is destined to keep up his perfect luck for eternity. It is, indeed, hell. No one wants to catch a fish every time he casts a flyline.

We hadn't done very well, and on our second day we gained some wisdom from one of the Welsh anglers, who reacted to the air of depression we must have exhibited as we climbed into our boat. Unless in competition mode, I have found that all fishermen – who wonder at this sport of ours that is so addictive – have a common bond, regardless of nationality: to share experiences and knowledge for the greater good of all his fellow fisherman. He gave us the real deal: a fly that would work for us. It was two sizes bigger than the ones we had unsuccessfully used the day before, with a green iridescent back where ours had none. Fished dry, they were easy to see, being quite big, so 'takes' would be easy to spot. Or so we thought. Fishing is never quite what you expect, and it is futile to think that it will be, but we still go on expecting something, even if it is futile – for we are fishermen! Beetles, a lot of them, were on the surface of the water, but in the ripple, the flies on our lines just disappeared. The trout sucked them into their mouths without showing any trace that they had done so. Of course, this realisation came only in retrospect, when our rods started to bend with no evidence that the trout had actually taken our fly. This meant that many more would have been unseen as they tried and swiftly rejected our fly, realising that it wasn't what they were looking for before the hook took hold, and us none the wiser.

There are certainly more visible ways for a trout to take your fly. The head and tailer is a trout almost out of the water, head bearing down on the surface fly, then tail following. Sometimes a neb (nose) can be spotted breaking the surface as it eats a fly, and sometimes a boil near the fly means that the fish has refused the fly at the last moment. However, that could also mean it simply missed it and, if you wait, the fish will sometimes make an adjustment and have another go, then suddenly the boil is where the fly was, and the fish is hooked. There can be no more exciting, adrenaline-filled fishing experience than a fish taking a dry fly. Too often things happen that seem indecipherable, incomprehensible: I can spend a long time looking at my dry fly and there it remains, doing nothing special, perhaps bobbing a bit in the ripple or wave, and when I look away, eyes drawn momentarily elsewhere, Sod's law has it this is when the fish hits the fly and there it is, on my line or not (depending on whether the hook has gained its purchase in the fish's mouth). It happens too much to be classed as accidental or flukish – there is something ineffable at work, beyond the minds of mere fishermen. It is a mystery that will remain forever unsolved.

The fishermen on Clywedog were friendly, amicable and pleasant, though we didn't know them – raising an arm in acknowledgement and shouting across the water, "How are you doing?". This isn't always the case elsewhere. In other places I have fished, fishermen seem to be more insular, though willing enough to talk to you if you are known to them. In my first England final eliminator on Grafham Water, I was paired with a well-known Midlands angler. I caught two trout but didn't qualify, and he blanked. Four or five trout were needed on that day, as twenty or so others also caught two (one day I fished an English final eliminator on a reservoir in Sussex where over half the competitors, fifty anglers, didn't catch, so catching two on that day would give you a chance of qualifying for the England team – I caught one!) Knowing no one, before I left, I sought him out to wish him well and thank him for his company, but he was amongst his friends and seemed to be totally thrown by my actions – even embarrassed – and I felt I had committed an immense faux pas. Our eight hours together on the boat just didn't merit these rudimentary niceties. Competition fishing has an etiquette that is soon learnt: don't try to get to know your partner. You won't meet again, and no one appreciates extraneous chit-chat. If your partner is catching and you are not, and you ask what fly he has caught on, well, no angler in a competition will treat your request as anything as a sign of weakness, and why should he respond? What if, having been given the fly pattern, you outfish him, his team is also affected by your success, and they finish in an inferior position? No, expect a taciturn answer, and the name of a different fly pattern completely.

That second day on Clywedog eclipsed the first, and not just in its better catch rate. The weather was kinder, the wind not so strong and also warmer: a southerly. We watched red kites flying no more than 100 meters high above us. They are a magnificent bird, but not rare around here. Not far away a local farmer feeds them, and they can number several hundred at this feeding station, so they have recovered from their near extinction.

My stories here have mostly recounted the best fishing that I have experienced in great places. What of the other days, the bad times and disappointments? Well, there are plenty of those. Looking back at the places we fished, there were some that we wasted a whole lot of time and money on. Iceland, spectacular as it was, could be said to be such a place, as far as fishing goes, anyway. We arrived after researching a river (I forget its name, but I know I found it unpronounceable) that was supposedly the home of large wild brown trout, and we were eager to get amongst the action. But we realised after a few days that the river was empty. Andrew walked its entire length, about six miles, to where it emptied into the sea, and even using fish-spotting skills honed in New Zealand, never spotted any fish. We discovered a spot, an adjunct to the river itself, enclosed by wire netting, where large grown-on brown trout with stunted tails and malformed fins were reared, and presumably released into the river for some unlucky angler to catch and wonder what was going on! Our mistake: never believe the promotional blurb, always seek out someone who has fished there. There were compensations – Iceland was a land of wonderment: geysers, waterfalls, hot springs and glaciers, and the best lamb I have ever tasted – due, I think, to the herbs and mosses that they fed on.

I have learned a lot in my fishing trips to different lands. Travel opens up one's mind, and it was my trip to Wyoming and Montana that taught me the American Indians (known only to me previously as the bad guys at the battle of Little Big Horn) had 'right' on their side, fighting to correct an injustice put upon them by the US government. I went to the Whanganui, a river on the North Island of New Zealand, to fish, but also learnt the history of the Maoris that lived around this river for centuries. The Maoris consider the Whanganui River an ancestor, and in 2017 it was designated the legal status of a person, granting in law what the Maoris had been insisting all along: the river is a living being. Its new status means if someone abuses or harms it, the law sees no differentiation between harming the tribe and harming the river, because they are one and the same. Two Guardians are appointed to act on behalf of the Whanganui River, one from the Crown and one from the Maori tribe of Iwi. Responding to the new legislation, the Government issued an apology for its historical wrongdoing, acknowledging that it had breached a treaty, undermined the ability of Whanganui tribes to exercise their customary rights and responsibilities in respect of the river, and compromised their physical, cultural and spiritual well-being.

This is the river that for more than 700 years the Whanganui tribes controlled, cared for, and depended on, but when European settlers arrived in the mid-1800s, the tribe's traditional authority was undermined and finally extinguished by government decree. Since then, the Maoris have watched their river being degraded and disgraced, even as it was feted as a scenic wonder – 'the Rhine of New Zealand'. It became a drain for the city's effluent, and a sprawling hydroelectric power scheme deprived the river of much of the flow in its upper reaches. The river rises in the snowfields of a trio of volcanos in central north island. One of them, Ngauruhoe, is the mythical Mount Doom in Peter Jackson's film adaptations of *Lord of the Rings*. The river is now celebrated and revered once more, but its new status doesn't alter the fact that it is not owned by the Maoris as it once was, just as the Sioux in North America have never regained the Black Hills, ceded to them in a treaty which the United States government then broke. I fished the Whanganui River with little success – I hooked just a few small browns, seeking sanctuary close to the bank of a river raging with floodwaters – but you learn to accept that nature will thwart you.

What more of my disasters or less successful outcomes? Fishing a mountain lake for brown trout in mid-Wales, it took me three trips before I even wet a line. This was a new lake I wanted to fish, so I went to reconnoitre it. Up a mountain track only suitable for 4x4's (and I didn't own one of those) I found it easily enough, but there was another lake, they said, just a little further on, so I thought 'let's see what that's like?' Fifteen miles later (for I completely missed this second lake), through a forest, following an almost undrivable track churned up by huge lorries with their cargo of tree-trunks, I came with relief to a tarmac road, good only for heading home. The second trip to the mountain lake, I walked down towards the water and strayed unwittingly into a bog from which it took some hours to extricate myself. Exhausted from pulling out my legs, sinking sometimes to my knees, I had no desire and no strength left to fish. I know now how to recognise boggy terrain. Finally, on the third trip, I fished the lake and caught a beautifully marked brown trout, but my, it was cold that day. I headed for home.

When I was younger, I used to fish in the coldest of weathers – at times the ice would freeze the flyline to the rod-rings – but no more. You sort of get over that silliness, or maybe you just grow up! The only time I ever had a dunking was when I was fishing Mula Reservoir in Spain with two friends. I was standing on a rock that I thought was stable, and then I was in the water along with the rock. My companions were some way away, but Roger had seen me go under and rushed over with dry towels. Roger told me afterwards that Ray, who had been fishing next to him, simply said: "I think he'll get out alright". Some friends look out more for you than others!

Fishing days are always eventful: days when your wet-weather gear doesn't live up to its name and you come in soaked. Days when the wind-chill makes a mockery of your so-called thermals and you shiver. Days when you wonder whether there are any fish in the water. Red-letter days because of the quantity of fish you caught, or because it was just great to be where you were, or because you caught a beautiful fish. Days when fishing doesn't sooth the savage breast and days when it does. Days of utter disaster when you break a rod or mangle a fly line. Days when somehow you lose your number one fly box overboard and you ask the rangers constantly in the forlorn hope that they have found it – it is supposed to float – and of course, they haven't. Days when you can't get the outboard motor to start, no matter how much you yank the starter cord, and your arm is almost pulled out of its socket with the effort it takes. Days when time seems to have been suspended, and days also when time speeds up, and the light has somehow vanished, and you are heading home far too soon. Days when no matter what you do, you are fishless and puzzled and disappointed. Days when the sheer beauty of a sunset or sunrise on the water takes your breath away. Days when your fly box is entirely denuded of flies, due to you losing them inside fish, broken off, or the hook straightened, meaning a long session at the fly-tying vice. Days when you lose your car keys (it happened to me in Montana). Days (lots of them) of drinking too much wine and enjoying others' company at the expense of the fishing. Days, oh, those rare days, when you enter the zone and fish above your normal constraints and skills, entering into a pact with the angling gods and, this time around, you are successful.

EPILOGUE

I was born into the generation referred to as the baby boomers. Today, when this world of ours is riven with uncertainty and strife, I am grateful to have been part of this time. It was a golden era, free from what had gone before – two World Wars had cursed previous generations – and healthier, due to the creation of the NHS and medical advances. Freedoms were unchallenged by what we refer to today as the climate crisis, or carbon footprints, because we knew no better. Some research just a few decades ago even pointed towards a new Ice Age, before climate scientists researched and described global warming. Generations now have to deal with this problem, whilst we lived in blissful ignorance. As I grew older I became aware that I was an unwitting contributor to the change – albeit in a small role – by flying around the globe, increasing my carbon footprint and helping to undermine the places where I loved to fish. I regarded them as pristine wildernesses, and took long-haul flights to places like Thailand and the Maldives for holidays. I don't think we can justify doing this anymore. David Attenborough and his team may have clocked up millions of air miles, but in doing so they have educated us in the natural world and, through that, enlightened us all about this endangered planet we share.

Would I do this all again, would I just ignore the science and go? I'm too old, really, to expend the necessary energy and put up with jet lag, but what if I wasn't, and could go again to New Zealand or America? The simple answer is "I don't know", because I have had some amazing experiences in wonderful places. Perhaps I would try to repeat them. But I also know that fishing a Welsh mountain lake for wild brown trout near my home can match many of those experiences, and this now scratches my itch to go further afield.

In his biography *A River Runs Through It*, Norman Maclean ends with an elegiac and haunting piece of writing which it isn't possible to better:

> Eventually, all things merge into one, and a river runs through it. The river was cut by the worlds great flood and runs over rocks from the basement of time. On some of the rocks are timeless raindrops. Under the rocks are the words, and some of the words are theirs. I am haunted by waters.

ACKNOWLEDGEMENTS

It would be remiss of me not to mention friends and family members that helped enormously in providing encouragement and support, and my fellow fishermen that helped finesse the fishing tales that are part of this book. In particular, I would like to thank my daughter, Sara Wheeler, who was always a source of positivity, and Roger Honess, a fisherman friend whose encouragement was so important in the early days of writing this book. My thanks also to Peter Gulliford, my ex business partner and friend – and no mean fisherman himself – who took on the extra work burden whilst I went fishing, and a huge 'thank you' must go to Charlotte Fleming, my editor, who managed to create some sense out of my scribblings.

Also, my gratitude always to my dear, sweet brother in law, Terry Spratley, who has recently passed away, and who lent comedic value at the beginning of this book in pretending to behave as a trout would once hooked, and who gave me every encouragement to become a fly fisherman.

Finally, my eternal thanks to Ann, to whom this book is dedicated, and who had no inkling when we first met that I would spend so much time on this adopted sport of mine, but who was always prepared to listen a sympathetic ear to my tales of woe relating to my fishing exploits!

GLOSSARY OF TERMS

Anadromous

Species of fish that migrate up rivers from the sea to breed.

Barbless

A hook with the barb removed or flattened, essential for catch and release.

Breaking strain

Refers to the breaking strain of nylon used in leaders and it is determined by the breakage obtained when a certain weight is lifted and the nylon breaks.

Buzzer

A common term for the larval stage of the chironomid.

Chalk stream

UK term for a limestone river.

Chironomid

A group of insects which have three life stages. The non-biting midges are called buzzers by fly fishers.

Dropper

An additional fly on a leader, can be tied inline or as a spur.

Dry Fly

Any pattern which sits on the surface of the water.

Emerger

An imitation of a natural fly which is half in the surface of the water and half out.

Figure eight

A retrieve style that gives a smooth, steady movement to the fly.

Flyline

A 30 Metre length of line which has a braided core and a PVC coating that facilitates casting of a fly by propelling it forward. Originally from horsehair, then made from silk. One end is connected to the Reel, the other has a nylon leader attached to it.

Fritz

A chenille used in fly tying made from tinsel.

Hackle

Feather which is wound around the hook shank.

Leader

A thin diameter of nylon that attaches to the fly line that can be various lengths from nine feet to as much as twenty five feet to which the fly or flies are tied to.

Lough

A large lake in Ireland. In Scotland, they are called lochs.

Lure

A pattern that is not really imitative – it deceives or attracts curiosity or aggression.

Marabou

A highly mobile feather fibre from the marabou stork but now sourced from the common Turkey.

Nymph

A tying which suggests the larval stage of aquatic life.

Stockies

The term used for trout when they are stocked from a fish farm into a water and are not wild fish.

Terrestrials

Insects that originate on land but fall onto water such as hawthorn, ant, daddy-long-legs and beetles.

Wet Fly

Refers to any fly fished below the surface but specifically to the older group of winged and hackled wet flies such as The Butcher, Dunkeld or Peter Ross.

REFERENCES & RECOMMENDATIONS

Claudius Aelianus, *De Natura Animalium, On the Characteristics of Animals*, 1784

Dame Juliana Berners, *A Treatyse of Fysshynge with an Angle (The Boke of St Albans)*, William Pickering, 1827

Bill Bryson, *The Body, A Guide for Occupants*, Transworld Publishers Ltd, 2019

Henry Cholmondeley-Pennel, *The Classic Guide to Fly Fishing*, Amberley Publishing Limited, 2015

Charles Dickens, *A Tale of Two Cities*

Renni Eddo-Lodge, *Why I'm No Longer Talking to White People About Race*, Bloomsbury Circus, 2017)

Ralph Waldo Emerson , *Emerson in His Journals*, Belknap Press, 1982

John Gierach, *A Fly Rod of Your Own*, Simon & Schuster, 2017

John Gierach, *Dances with Trout*, Simon & Schuster, 2005

Indeed anything by John Gierach

Frederic Halford, *Floating Flies and How to Dress Them: A Treatise on the Most Modern Methods of Dressing Artificial Flies for Trout and Grayling*, Creative Media Partners, 2017

Ernest Hemingway, *The Old Man and the Sea*, 1952

Bruce Hood, *The Self Illusion, Why There is No 'You' Inside Your Head*, Constable, 2012

Washington Irving, The Complete World of Washington Irving, Kindle, 2017

Daniel Kahneman, Amos Tversky, *Thinking Fast and Slow*, Penguin, 2012

Rudyard Kipling, *If (poem)*

Jiddu Krishnamurti, *Freedom From the Known*, Ebury Publishing, 2010

Jiddu Krishnamurti, *The Network of Thought*, Harper & Row Publishers, 1983

Charles Lamb, Jr., Mary Anne Lamb. *The Letters of Charles and Mary Anne Lamb 1796–1801*, Cornell University Press, 1975

Norman MacLean, *A River Runs Through It*, University of Chicago Press, 1976

Riccardo Manzotti, *The Spread Mind Theory: Why Conciousness and the World are One*, OR Books, 2018

Albert Jules McClane, *The Compleat McClane: A Treasury of A.J. McClane's Classic Angling Adventures.* E.P. Dutton, 1988

Tim Parks, *Teach Us to Sit Still: A Sceptic's Search for Health and Healing,* Harvill Secker, 2010

Tim Parks, *Out of My Head: On the Trail of Consciousness,* Harvill Secker, 2018

Tom Rosenbauer, *The Orvis Guide to Essential American Flies,* Lyons Press, 2021

Philip Roth, *The Human Stain,* Vintage, 2001

Frank Sawyer, *Keeper of the Stream,* Adam and Charles Black, 1952

Kathryn Schulz, *Being Wrong: Adventures in the Margin of Error,* Ecco, 2010

John Steinbeck, *The Grapes of Wrath*

Will Storr, *Selfie: How We Became So Self-Obsessed and What It's Doing to Us,* Picador, 2017

Ajahn Sumedho, *The Mind and the Way,* Wisdom Publications, 1995

Eckhart Tolle, *The Power of Now,* Yellow Kite, 2001

Mark Twain, *The Innocents Abroad*

Izaak Walton, *The Compleat Angler,* Bell and Daldy, 1863

Articles

J D Rose, R Arlinghaus, S J Cooke, B K Diggles, W Sawynok, E D Stevens, C D L Wynne. 'Can fish really feel pain?' *Fish and Fisheries,* 2012; DOI: 10.1111/faf.12010

Kimbra Cutlip, 'In 1868, Two Nations Made a Treaty, the U.S. Broke It and Plains Indian Tribes are Still Seeking Justice' *Smithsonian Magazine,* 2018; https://www.smithsonianmag.com/smithsonian-institution/1868-two-nations-made-treaty-us-broke-it-and-plains-indian-tribes-are-still-seeking-justice-180970741/

Lightning Source UK Ltd.
Milton Keynes UK
UKHW022104240622
404937UK00006B/83